The Online Business Academy for Beginners

A Comprehensive and Proven Guide to Start and Build a Profitable Online Business That Generates 15k Passive Income Months with the Best Operations in Place

Written By:

Thomas Bourne

Contents

© **Copyright 2023 Thomas Bourne - All Rights Reserved.**

The content contained within this book may not be reproduced, duplicated or transmitted without direct written permission from the author or the publisher.

Under no circumstances will any blame or legal responsibility be held against the publisher, or author, for any damages, reparation, or monetary loss due to the information contained within this book. Either directly or indirectly.

Legal Notice:

This book is copyright protected. This book is only for personal use. You cannot amend, distribute, sell, use, quote or paraphrase any part, or the content within this book, without the consent of the author or publisher.

Disclaimer Notice:

Please note the information contained within this document is for educational and entertainment purposes only. All effort has been executed to present accurate, up to date, and reliable, complete information. No warranties of any kind are declared or implied. Readers acknowledge that the author is not engaging in the rendering of legal, financial, medical or professional advice. The content within this book has been derived from various sources. Please consult a licensed professional before attempting any techniques outlined in this book.

By reading this document, the reader agrees that under no circumstances is the author responsible for any losses, direct or indirect, which are incurred as a result of the use of the information contained within this document, including, but not limited to, — errors, omissions, or inaccuracies.

Contents

Introduction	1
Chapter One: Is Online Business for You?	7
The Internet Today	7
What is an online business?	9
The History of Online Business	11
Impact of Online Businesses on Society	16
The Future of E-Commerce	17
Benefits of the Internet for Businesses	20
Different Types of Online Businesses	33
Online Business Myths You Should Discard	39
Key Takeaways	41
Chapter Two: Online Business Ideas	43
10 Most Lucrative Online Businesses	43
10 Online Businesses You Can Start with No Money	48

50 Other Online Business Ideas　　　　　　　　　　　51

　　Profitable Niches in the Online Business　　　　　　63

　　Choosing the Best Online Business for You　　　　　70

　　Understanding Online Business Models　　　　　　　72

　　Tips for Choosing a Successful Online Business　　　75

　　Successful Online Businesses You Can Learn From　76

　　Key Takeaways　　　　　　　　　　　　　　　　　　85

Chapter Three: Cultivating an Entrepreneurial Mindset　87

　　How Viable is Your Business　　　　　　　　　　　　90

　　Conducting Product and Market Research　　　　　　94

　　How to Start Creating a Domain Name and Website　98

　　Identifying your Target Market (Analyzing the Market)　103

　　Writing a Strategic Business Plan　　　　　　　　　106

　　Examine the Competition　　　　　　　　　　　　　109

　　Determining your Business Structure　　　　　　　　114

　　Considerations When Choosing a Business Structure　120

　　Knowing the Legalities Involved　　　　　　　　　　122

Chapter Four: Accounting and Financing　　　　　125

　　Startups Costs　　　　　　　　　　　　　　　　　　125

　　Creating a Budget　　　　　　　　　　　　　　　　129

　　Managing Your Personal Finance　　　　　　　　　134

Contents

How Feasible is Bootstrapping? ... 137

Other Forms of Funding Your Business ... 138

Are there Shortcuts to Funding Your Online Business? ... 141

Your Revenue Structure ... 142

Taxes on Online Business ... 146

Managing Your Tax Bracket ... 148

Managing Your Inventory ... 151

Software that Makes Accounting Easy ... 154

Should You Hire a Professional ... 160

Key takeaways ... 165

Chapter Five: How to Put Yourself Out There ... 167

Launching your New Online Business ... 167

E-commerce or Creating Your Domain Name ... 172

Adding New Products to your Online Store ... 176

Equipping Yourself with the Necessary Software Tools ... 180

Creating Visibility (Getting your First Clients) ... 183

Copywriting: An Important Tool ... 186

How to Establish your Reputation ... 188

The Power of Networking ... 191

Branding: A Crucial Part of Online Businesses ... 192

Key takeaways ... 195

Chapter 6: Marketing: Driving Growth and Sales   197

    The Power of SEO   198

    The Magic of Web Push Notifications   203

    Email Marketing: Turning Visitors into Buyers   207

    Other Strategies to Promote Your Online Business   211

    Content vs. Social Media vs. Email Marketing   213

    Understanding Time-Sensitive Promotions   218

    Developing a Winning Online Marketing Strategy   220

    Customer Relations is Key to Your Success   222

    Key takeaways   226

Chapter Seven: Value Proposition for Improved Profits   227

    Understanding Online Value Proposition (OVP)   228

    Key Techniques for Managing OVPs   242

    10 of the Best E-Commerce Value Propositions   244

    Key takeaways   248

Chapter Eight: Staying in Business   251

    Analyzing Your Performance   251

    Knowing When to Expand or Change Products   255

    Monitoring Your KPIs   258

    Back End Sales and Upselling   262

Contents

20 Tips for Staying in Business	263
Retaining and Satisfying Your Customers	266
Key takeaways	270

Conclusion — **273**

References — **277**

Introduction

Starting an online business often proves daunting, especially for people with no expertise or understanding in the area. You may have experimented with several side hustles or even fantasized about leaving your day job to start an online business and become your own boss. But the idea of creating a website, choosing a niche, identifying the correct target audience, and developing a viable business model might seem daunting.

Let me tell you about Derek. He was one of a kind. Derek aimed high. He aspired to be his own boss and achieve success in life. As a result, when he decided to launch an online business, he was filled with excitement and the passion for seeing it thrive. One day, Derek was watching a YouTube video when he saw an advertisement about Amazon FBA. He thought this must be the perfect online opportunity he was looking for. He decided to do more research about Amazon FBA. Some of the folks he read about were Amazon FBA merchants who were successful in their businesses. He was determined to be like them.

However, things didn't go as smoothly as he thought. He was disappointed with the lack of success after months of trying. He had put in many hours of effort but could not see any tangible

results.

A friend of Derek's invited him to a business conference since he had heard him talk about his dream and passion for starting an online business. He attended the conference with great enthusiasm. He felt a glimmer of hope as he listened to the speaker. He began to think that maybe if he followed the speaker's advice, he could make his dreams come true.

Derek approached the speaker after the session, anxious to learn more. That was when he met me, the author of *The Online Business Academy for Beginners*.

You see, that speaker was me. I took Derek under my wing and showed him the right way to launch an online business and how to build momentum and increase his earnings. I demonstrated how to determine his target audience and craft a convincing message with an irresistible offer for them. I assisted him in developing a conversion-optimized website and showed him how to utilize digital marketing tools to reach prospective clients.

Most significantly, I explained to him that anyone could succeed with the right mindset, follow a proven system that works, and consistently put in the required effort. I encouraged him to persevere in the face of adversity and never

Introduction

to give up on his aspirations. He would later go on to make multiple six and seven figures from his online businesses.

Many would identify with Derek's story. When reaching our objectives, we've all experienced frustration and uncertainty. However, anything is achievable with the right mentorship and corresponding effort.

That's why I created *The Online Business Academy for Beginners*. It's a step-by-step guide to launching and growing an internet business. In this book, I discuss all the methods and tactics I employed to assist Derek and a host of other students in building and operating successful businesses.

The Online Business Academy for Beginners is for you if you want an easy-to-follow strategy for moving your online business to the next level. This book will be your worthy guide whether you have never launched a business before or are a new business owner. It will help you clarify your business objectives, develop a plan of action, and make your ideas a reality.

You are not alone. You are part of a rising group of persons who want financial independence, creative satisfaction, and the ability to work on their terms. The internet world has limitless prospects for enterprise and advancement, but navigating it may be difficult, especially for beginners.

The Online Business Academy for Beginners can help with this. This detailed guide was developed with you in mind – the budding entrepreneur looking to realize their aspirations. Whether you want to establish a new business or grow an existing one, this book will provide you with the information, skills, and tools you need to succeed.

In this book, I'll show you how to:

- Create a detailed and successful business strategy.

- Choose the best niche for your business.

- Create a website that turns visitors into paying clients.

- Increase your online presence and traffic.

- Make your website search engine friendly.

- Create and advertise items that your target market will appreciate.

- Monetize your website with advertising, affiliate marketing, and other income sources.

- Manage your money and expand your business.

- And more

This book is more than a how-to manual for kick-starting an online business. It is based on my wealth of experience and success in operating several successful online businesses and the most recent industry studies and trends. I am a successful entrepreneur, Amazon FBA bestseller, award-winning digital

Introduction

marketer, and educator who has assisted hundreds of people and companies achieve their online marketing goals. With a business background and a love for internet marketing, I believe I am in the best position to guide and help you launch or grow your online business.

See what some readers thought of this book.

"I just completed the final chapter of Online Business Academy for Beginners. It was a fantastic read! I learned a lot about starting my own online business. I appreciated the extensive instructions on how to earn more than $15,000 per month on Amazon FBA and drop shipping. I strongly recommend this book to anybody interested in starting their own online business." - Alex. S.

"I just finished reading the book Online Business Academy for Beginners and was quite pleased. It is a very detailed and simple guide to launching an internet business. The step-by-step directions on how to earn good income monthly online were extremely beneficial. I'm delighted I read this book, and I will be recommending it to friends who wish to make money doing business online." - Mia. J.

The Online Company Academy for Beginners is an in-depth book that will guide you through the process of beginning and expanding your online business. Thanks to practical suggestions, effective tactics, and real-life examples, this book will give you the confidence and skills you need to transform your business goals.

So, if you're ready to take your business to the next level, this book is for you. The Online Company Academy for Beginners is the perfect resource for anybody wishing to establish and create a successful online business. With its clear, straightforward, and proactive approach, it will be easy for you to grasp and implement the ideas I shared in the book. Prepare to embark on a voyage of discovery, learning, and development that will transform your life.

Chapter One

Is Online Business for You?

The Internet Today

The Internet is a global computer network that connects using predefined communication protocols. It allows people from all over the world to communicate with one another. The Internet is sometimes known as the World Wide Web or just the Web. It has come a long way from its inception in the 1950s. It was initially intended to enable government organizations, universities, and military units to share information and engage with each other. The first successful communication via the internet was sent on October 29, 1969, between two computers at UCLA and the Stanford Research Institute.

The Internet was originally used by the scientific and academic organization. However, as it became more accessible and user-friendly, many individuals, businesses, and organizations started to adopt it. Users could access and exchange information and resources far more quickly once the World Wide Web was introduced in 1991. The World Wide Web is a network-based system of linked hypertext pages and multimedia data.

Is Online Business for You?

Today, business operations have been profoundly impacted by the advent of the Internet. Online businesses are becoming more common, and online customers have increased dramatically. Businesses can reach customers all over the globe thanks to the proliferation of e-commerce websites. Doing internet business also helps companies save money on operating expenses since they do not need physical stores.

Amazon, Amazon.com, an online bookstore founded in 1995, was one of the earliest internet businesses. Amazon revolutionized book buying before expanding to include electronics, clothing, and home items. Today, Amazon is the world's largest and most popular e-commerce platform, making online shopping easy and convenient for millions of consumers worldwide.

The expansion of e-commerce has also benefitted small businesses and entrepreneurs. Many small businesses can now reach a global audience and compete with larger firms. Etsy, for example, is a global online marketplace where small businesses may sell handmade products and crafts to customers worldwide.

The rise of social media is another way the Internet has changed business operations. Social media platforms such as Facebook, Twitter, and LinkedIn have advanced into effective marketing and advertising tools for businesses. Many businesses are now using these platforms to reach new customers, communicate with existing ones, and promote their brands. Social media has also made it easier for businesses to get customer feedback and respond to their needs.

The expansion of mobile devices has also significantly impacted

online businesses. With the increased popularity of smartphones and tablets, many people are utilizing their mobile devices to access the Internet and make online purchases. This has created new opportunities for businesses to reach out to customers on the go and made it easier for individuals to buy from anywhere.

If you want to start an online business, you will discover a plethora of possibilities on the Internet. The Internet gives you access to a global audience, helping you reach millions of potential customers without ever leaving your home. You may also save on operating costs since you won't have to maintain a physical storefront. Furthermore, the Internet provides access to various tools and information, making it easier to establish and grow your business. From marketing and advertising to e-commerce platforms and payment processors, the Internet has everything you need to start an online business. So, why not take advantage of all the Internet has to offer and start your online business right now?

What is an online business?

Is Online Business for You?

Online business is any kind of business that is done primarily via the Internet and other digital technology. This form of business, often known as e-commerce, is now more popular than ever because of its ease, affordability, and scalability.

The backbone of every successful online business is a functional website, a collection of linked pages where visitors may learn about and purchase a business's goods and services. Businesses that operate solely online utilize the web for everything from gathering leads to handling client payments. Many e-commerce sites allow users to make purchases without ever having to set foot in a shop.

Several factors must work together well for an online company to succeed. First and foremost, you must have a well-designed, user-friendly, and search-engine-optimized website. Also, it must provide a safe method of payment and detailed information about the company's offerings. The website must also include a user-friendly shopping cart and customer care system to facilitate fast responses to inquiries and order processing.

Content marketing is another crucial aspect of internet business. To attract and keep clients, online businesses use a strategy known as "content marketing." Content like blog entries, articles, videos, podcasts, and social media posts all count towards building a successful online business. Lead generation and customer connection building are two primary goals of any successful marketing strategy, and content marketing helps achieve both.

Finally, a strong online presence is essential for every business operating online. This implies making a significant impact on sites like Facebook, Twitter, and Instagram. To increase online visibility, businesses should also strive to appear on popular review sites like Yelp and search engines like Google and Bing.

Overall, running an online business is a fantastic way for

entrepreneurs to have access to customers all around the world. Remember that launching an online business differs from running a typical brick-and-mortar firm. You need accurate information, proper guidance, and a setup to start on the right foot. Is there a history behind the online business? Let's find out.

The History of Online Business

Pre-Internet Era - The Evolution of Electronic Commerce

Online business boomed in the 1990s and 2000s, but its roots can be traced back to the gradual but steady growth of electronic trade in the pre-Internet era. Although widespread access to the internet was still years away, several companies and institutions were already dabbling with electronic methods of doing business. In this period, B2B (business-to-business) transactions were the primary focus of electronic commerce, which relied on specialized networks and mainframe computers.

Is Online Business for You?

Electronic Data Interchange (EDI) was implemented in the late 1960s and early 1970s, making it one of the first instances of electronic commerce. Electronic data interchange was a common communication protocol for exchanging business documents like invoices and purchase orders between corporations and their trading partners. As a result, businesses could minimize the time spent on manual data input while boosting accuracy, productivity, and streamlining operations. EDI swiftly gained widespread adoption among major organizations and is now utilized in many different sectors, including manufacturing, retail, and the financial industry.

The adoption of EFT (Electronic funds transfer) systems, which are used to transfer money digitally, was another early innovation in online trade. Electronic money transfers between bank accounts were made possible by these technologies, which both corporations and people used. As a result, the time and money spent processing financial transactions were greatly lessened, making this a vast improvement over the previous system of physically sending checks or money orders. In the 1970s and 1980s, EFT systems rose in popularity and became used by various financial institutions, including banks, businesses, and government organizations.

The introduction of minicomputers and personal computers in the late 1970s and early 1980s ushered in a new era of electronic business. As a result of their size and price, these computers were available to a larger variety of organizations and people than mainframe computers. This led to the launching of innovative programs and apps for streamlining corporate procedures. One example is the proliferation of computerized accounting and inventory systems, as well as the use of electronic forms of communication like email by many companies to interact with their clients and vendors.

Despite these developments, consumers still could not participate in online shopping since it was primarily used for business-to-business transactions. Midway through the 1980s, however, the first online services providers like CompuServe, Prodigy, and America Online emerged, and things began to change. These services made access to data, emails, and online discussion groups possible, while companies gained a fresh channel through which to connect with consumers.

Software Etc., a software retailer, launched an online shop on CompuServe in 1985, making it one of the first companies to use internet services. To say that this was a game-changing innovation that ushered in a new age of e-commerce would be an understatement. After that, other stores started selling items online, and the trend continued. While internet services were still in their infancy, many companies saw the enormous potential of doing business online and started to spend heavily on creating an online presence.

Early E-commerce Platforms

The advent of the World Wide Web (WWW) and graphical web browsers like Mosaic and Netscape Navigator in the 1990s lowered the barrier to entry for regular internet users. This was a watershed moment in online purchasing history, as

Is Online Business for You?

companies could suddenly connect with customers globally and provide them with a more exciting and personalized buying experience.

The proliferation of online shops parallels the development of the web. The late 1990s saw the rise of internet shopping, and many conventional stores struggled to compete. The internet leveled the playing field for businesses of all sizes, and it allowed startups to join the market and compete with well-established names. This prompted fast innovation and the establishment of new business models, such as business-to-consumer (B2C) e-commerce platforms like Amazon.com and online marketplaces like eBay.com.

Because of the proliferation of online retailers and consumers, innovative payment methods and technologies also emerged. When internet shopping became popular, only established payment systems like credit cards were accepted. However, as the internet expanded, new payment methods like PayPal appeared, streamlining the process of making online purchases.

Before the development of internet security measures, doing business online was fraught with difficulty. There was apprehension about the safety of online purchases. So shoppers were hesitant to provide sensitive information such as credit card numbers and bank account details. Corporations and organizations created new security protocols and technologies, like encryption and secure socket layer (SSL) certificates, in response to these concerns.

Despite the difficulties and limitations of the pre-Internet era, electronic commerce developed during this time, paving the way for the expansion and success of online businesses in the years that followed. Technologies like electronic data interchange (EDI) and electronic funds transfer (EFT) were among the first to pave the way for further innovations in e-commerce. Businesses and entrepreneurs found a new, fast-growing market in the '90s and '00s. Thanks to the proliferation of the internet and the rise of online shopping.

Rise of Online Businesses

The growth of online businesses has been nothing short of

spectacular in recent years. The simplicity of online purchases and the widespread use of smartphones has resulted in considerable growth in the number of online companies. The tendency is certain to continue, particularly now that the COVID-19 epidemic has hastened the move to online purchasing and e-commerce.

The lower initial startup costs required are one of the primary drivers of expanding internet businesses. A website, social media presence, and digital marketing tools are all required to start an online company. Compare this to the costly expenses of leasing a physical shop or office space, paying staff, and purchasing merchandise. With the help of the internet, many entrepreneurs have launched their online businesses with very little cash.

Is Online Business for You?

Another key aspect contributing to the expansion of online commerce is the internet's global reach. Online businesses may reach clients all over the globe, creating a considerably broader market than brick-and-mortar firms, which are often constrained to their immediate surroundings. This has allowed internet enterprises to develop unprecedentedly and compete with bigger, more established brands.

Furthermore, online businesses benefit from the ability to gather massive volumes of data about their clients. This information may be utilized to obtain insights into consumer behavior, preferences, and purchase patterns, allowing you to enhance the customer experience and generate more successful marketing campaigns. Online businesses may also view their consumers' website activity, allowing them to enhance their site

and improve the customer experience.

Aside from these benefits, the emergence of social media has given internet-based businesses a great tool for increasing brand recognition and connecting with consumers. Social media sites such as Facebook, Instagram, and Twitter have made it easy for companies to engage with their target audience and grow a following.

Overall, online businesses have ushered in a new age of entrepreneurship and altered how people purchase and sell goods and services. As the trend continues, more businesses are likely to move online, resulting in a more competitive and dynamic market. Entrepreneurs who wish to profit from this trend must first understand the particular benefits and constraints of online enterprises and be prepared to adapt to the ever-changing digital world.

Impact of Online Businesses on Society

There are several ways in which the growth of internet enterprises has significantly influenced society. The increasing ease and availability of products and services are perhaps the most noticeable of these effects. Due to the convenience of online shopping, customers no longer have to fight crowds or adhere to stringent store hours. How individuals meet their basic needs and pursue their passions has revolutionized.

The economic effect of online business is substantial, and not

only because of the ease they provide. Online shopping's meteoric rise has opened up exciting new communication channels with consumers for businesses of all sizes. This resulted in a boost in competitiveness and spurred the creation of new employment, both of which have contributed to the expansion and improvement of the economy.

The rise of e-commerce has had several good effects on modern life but has also been linked to a few less desirable outcomes. For example, the fast rise of e-commerce has placed pressure on brick-and-mortar retailers, prompting some to shut down and others to struggle. This has contributed to the demise of many older shopping malls, which has hurt some populations of neighborhoods that relied on them.

An additional consequence of e-commerce is the expansion of cybercrime. Cybercriminals have developed sophisticated methods to steal sensitive information and funds as the number of individuals making purchases and doing business online continues to rise. Because of this, it's crucial that everyone, from companies to consumers, take active measures to ensure their online safety.

The Future of E-Commerce

The future of e-commerce is likely to be affected by various technological, customer behavior, and economic trends and changes. Experts in the field have identified many important themes expected to drive the development and evolution of e-commerce in the following years. However, it is impossible to forecast precisely what the future will look like.

The rapid advancement of mobile commerce is one of the most important factors shaping the future of online shopping. The increasing use of smartphones and other mobile devices as primary internet access points suggests an uptick in interest in e-commerce platforms optimized for such devices. As a result, new technologies and platforms will emerge to facilitate customers' online shopping experiences on their mobile devices.

The emergence of social commerce is another factor that will shape the future of online shopping. Social media sites like Facebook, Instagram, and Pinterest continue to grow in popularity, prompting companies to seek out novel approaches to promoting their products and services to clients. One method is to use social media to communicate with consumers and increase brand recognition; another is to include social media shopping experiences directly into social media platforms.

Increases in AI (artificial intelligence) and ML (machine language) are also likely to significantly impact the growth of the e-commerce industry in the years to come. Automation of messages like product suggestions, customer assistance, and even orders and payment processing is anticipated to result from the widespread use of these technologies. In addition to improving customers' online shopping experiences, this will also aid retailers in streamlining their operations and maximizing their profits.

The development of innovative payment systems like cryptocurrencies, digital wallets, and biometric verification techniques has also been predicted to drive the future of e-commerce. Customers will benefit from increased safety and convenience, and companies will be able to reach a wider audience and compete globally, thanks to these innovative payment options.

The growing need for individualization and adaptation is also a major factor determining the future of e-commerce.

Is Online Business for You?

Businesses are adapting to meet customers' demands for unique and individualized services by providing them with bespoke offerings such as special orders, suggestions, and even marketing initiatives. As businesses strive to forge closer ties with their clientele and set themselves apart from the pack, this pattern will likely continue to expand in the years ahead.

Finally, the rising significance of sustainability and environmental responsibility is predicted to affect the future of e-commerce. Businesses are expected to react to the growing environmental consciousness of their customers by providing more environmentally friendly goods and services and decreasing their carbon footprint. Possible actions include switching to renewable energy sources, reducing waste, and switching to more eco-friendly materials for use in manufacturing and shipping.

The future of e-commerce seems promising and ripe with new prospects, whether due to investments in new technology, using the power of personalization and customization, or embracing sustainability and environmental responsibility.

Benefits of the Internet for Businesses

The Internet has been a game-changer for businesses in the 21st century. It offers incredible advantages to businesses of all sizes and industries, allowing them to reach more customers, increase their profits, and stay ahead of the competition. Here are some of the benefits businesses have seen from using the Internet.

1. **Faster and easier communication**

The advent of the internet has altered how businesses interact with one another and their customers. It's a great way for companies to stay in touch with their staff, clients, customers, and partners while minimizing costs. Thanks to the internet, businesses can now reach out to a wide audience in a short time, all at once. Email, video chat, online meetings, and social media are some other ways they may interact.

By doing so, firms may respond to inquiries promptly and communicate data effortlessly among employees who reside in various physical locations. The internet also facilitates cross-company collaboration, boosting productivity and client satisfaction. By using the internet, companies may save money on travel expenses and lessen their environmental impact. Using the internet has made corporate communication simpler, quicker, and cheaper.

2. **Improved information sharing**

Thanks to the internet, what used to be a manual process for companies is now automated. With the advent of new technologies, businesses have quicker and easier access to information and may store and share data with employees, partners, and consumers. With the internet's lightning-fast speeds, companies can safely and quickly transmit and share massive volumes of data with their partners, customers, and employees. As a result of instantaneous information access and sharing, productivity and efficiency have increased.

Is Online Business for You?

The internet also allows businesses to gather and analyze data, improving their ability to make strategic business choices. In addition, businesses may utilize the web to advertise their products and services to a larger demographic and attract new customers. In addition, businesses may provide their clients with a more satisfying experience all around thanks to real-time online interaction. The internet has revolutionized the corporate world, making it more streamlined and profitable.

3. Business automation

One of the most valuable features of the internet for businesses is the ability to automate processes. Automation helps businesses save time and money by streamlining processes and maximizing efficiency. When it comes to client information, order details, stock levels, and other metrics crucial to running a company, automation is a huge advantage. Customer support, order tracking, financial management, advertising, and other tasks may all be automated with the help of the right automation technologies.

When businesses automate routine processes that formerly required human labor, they free up personnel to concentrate on the company's core strengths. Improving customer service and the overall customer experience may be achieved via automation since it enhances accuracy and decreases human error. Businesses can respond rapidly to environmental and market changes thanks to automation. With automation, organizations can more accurately gauge performance, pinpoint problem areas, and fine-tune their procedures. In a nutshell, business automation is a very effective method for doing all three of these things plus more.

4. High-speed connection and mobile internet

One of the greatest advantages of the internet for corporations is the availability of high-speed connections and mobile internet. Businesses may maintain constant communication with their clients, vendors, and associates because of this rapid, anywhere-access-to-the-internet capability. Email, company websites, and other business apps are now accessible from any location and device, thanks to the proliferation of high-speed internet and mobile web. Facilitating quicker communication, file-sharing, and commercial operations is a welcome side effect.

Furthermore, it aids companies in maintaining competitiveness by providing them with the means to access and use the same resources as their rivals while making quick judgments. In addition, modern technology has enabled firms to get data in near-real time, enabling better, more timely decision-making. Businesses wishing to interact with customers, suppliers, and partners while on the road might benefit from high-speed connections and mobile internet access. With the advent of mobile technology, they can stay in touch with clients through email and client databases and handle financial matters wherever they are. Mobile and high-speed internet access are two of the internet's most valuable features for commercial enterprises.

Is Online Business for You?

5. Innovative marketing strategies for expanding your client base

The Internet provides a myriad of options for companies to expand their clientele. Businesses increasingly rely on digital marketing strategies like social media and user-generated content to broaden their consumer base. Companies use cutting-edge marketing methods like retargeting, customization, and AI-driven advertising campaigns to further expand their clientele. Businesses may expand their clientele and foster loyalty among their clientele by catering to their specific needs via the material and services they provide. Companies may expand their customer base and increase sales by using the internet.

6. Increased new clients and customer engagement

It's no secret that the internet has helped businesses expand their customer bases and strengthen relationships with existing clientele. A business may expand its customer base and deepen its relationships with current clients via online marketing, social media, and websites. A company's online presence may advertise its goods and services, include testimonials from satisfied consumers, and foster connections with these individuals. You can keep customers interested via an engaging experience by creating online content. Internet-based platforms also provide prompt responses to consumer queries and suggestions, enhancing customer care quality. As a result of the sum of these parts, the company gains both new and loyal customers.

7. Better customer service

One of the most significant advantages of the internet for businesses is improved customer service. To better serve their clients, businesses may readily use the internet. You may quickly address questions and concerns from consumers and improve your standing with the public by using the internet. Customers may also use a business's website or social media page to learn more about the goods and services offered. As a result, businesses can better connect with their clientele, resulting in more revenue and happier clients.

8. Using the internet to manage corporate networks

Businesses can quickly and easily access and control their internal networks from any location. This paves the way for improved internal communication and cooperation and ensures that corporate networks can always accommodate cutting-edge technologies. In addition, businesses may give workers safe, remote access to company servers and other internal resources through any internet-connected device. This facilitates the smooth operation of business networks while also increasing their safety and reliability.

9. Cost Savings

Internet use has been linked to significant cost savings for commercial enterprises. Access to the internet allows businesses

to use money-saving, time-saving, and otherwise unavailable online tools and services. For instance, businesses may

Is Online Business for You?

broaden their horizons by forming relationships with clients and vendors from all over the globe without incurring astronomical expenses for things like transportation and communication. As a bonus, they may save money on costly software and hardware by using cloud-based data storage and sharing services. It is generally agreed that businesses may save money by utilizing the internet, which they can reinvest in other parts of their operations.

10. Enhanced workplace and business productivity

Internet technology has dramatically altered the commercial world. Enhanced workplace and corporate efficiency are major perks. The internet has given businesses access to many materials that streamline and simplify their operations. With the help of the internet, for instance, workers in various regions of the globe may instantly share information and work together. Due to this, decisions may now be made much more quickly and accurately than before. Additionally, many procedures and duties may be automated, giving firms more time and enabling people to concentrate on higher-value jobs. As a consequence, employees can focus on their jobs, and the company as a whole thrives.

11. Social Media

Due to the proliferation of high-speed online connections, social media has become a revolutionary tool for modern enterprises. Social networking sites like Facebook, Twitter, and LinkedIn have allowed businesses to communicate with and market to far larger audiences than ever before. For instance, a company may use social media to spread the word about its products or services, build its brand name recognition, and interact with its clientele. Aside from the obvious benefits of increased brand awareness and customer loyalty, this strategy also yields valuable information on what consumers want and expect from a product or service. More than that, social media may be a medium for customer support, letting companies respond instantly to questions or concerns. Overall, social media has provided a very effective channel through which businesses can interact with their clientele, build their reputation, and expand their customer base.

Is online business for me?

The truth is, there's no one-size-fits-all answer to the question of whether an online business is right for you. What may work well for someone else might not fit your unique circumstances and goals. But, certain factors can help you decide if starting an online business is worth pursuing.

Do you have a product or service that you're passionate about? Do you have the time and resources to launch and maintain an online business? Are there potential customers who would be interested in what you offer? Answering these questions honestly can help you decide if starting an online business is right for you.

However, if you're debating whether or not to launch an online business, my advice is simple: go for it! An online business can offer a range of benefits that are hard to find elsewhere.

Is Online Business for You?

Firstly, there's the convenience factor – with an online business, you can work from anywhere and anytime. You don't have to worry about the costs associated with renting a store or hiring employees. You can launch your business much more quickly and cheaply than a traditional brick-and-mortar setup. In addition, you can quickly reach customers worldwide, making it easy for you to scale up and start paying yourself sooner.

Lastly, an online business offers access to more data than ever, so you can make informed decisions about your business and track its progress more easily. Ultimately, an online business is an ideal way to start a venture that could unlock incredible opportunities for you. So go ahead and give it a try – we promise you won't regret it!

However, you also need to remember that success in the digital marketplace doesn't come easily. This is not a get-rich-quick scheme that will make you wealthy overnight. You can launch an online business, but it may take some time to start seeing results. Developing expertise and expanding your business is a time-consuming process; therefore, you must be patient while you do so.

Also, think about why you want to succeed. An online business can be both lucrative and difficult. You may find success in your online business if you are driven by opportunities for growth. A career in online business, however, may not be the greatest choice if financial gain is your only motivation.

How profitable is E-commerce?

E-commerce profitability has long been a source of concern for

entrepreneurs and businesses in the digital era. With the growth of technology and the internet, many businesses have taken advantage of the possibility to reach an unprecedented number of prospective customers. This has a tremendous influence on the profitability of e-commerce and has enabled businesses to increase their sales and earnings in a very short time.

The key to success in online business is learning what makes it unique. The reduced price is one of the key benefits of online shopping. The development of internet retail has allowed companies to avoid the high overhead of opening a physical storefront. This drastically decreases the expenses of operating an online company, making it much cheaper for businesses to join the e-commerce sector.

E-commerce also has the added benefit of being accessible to people worldwide. With the advent of the internet, companies have access to a global market. Since there will be more people who may potentially buy, it means more money for companies. E-commerce sites may also be used to focus on specialized audiences and niche markets, expanding the scope and efficiency of a business's outreach efforts.

The ease of use for consumers is also a major benefit of online shopping. Customers save time and energy by shopping online

Is Online Business for You?

since they can do so from the convenience of their own homes. Customers are more likely to be satisfied and loyal if they can more easily complete transactions. Businesses that are accessible around the clock stand to gain from their clients shopping whenever they choose.

Another benefit of e-commerce that might help firms raise revenues is the opportunity to monitor client information. By collecting customer data, organizations may acquire insights into client behavior, preferences, and interests. To maximize profits, this data may be utilized to develop more specific marketing strategies and boost conversion rates.

Overall, the e-commerce business is quite lucrative. It allows businesses to increase earnings and get an edge in the market by using the many benefits of online trading. Businesses may fully realize the promise of e-commerce if they have the proper strategy and technologies in place.

Why You Should Consider Starting an Online Business

Starting an online business is a great way to create additional income and have more control over your work-life balance. It can be a rewarding experience, both financially and personally, if done right. Here are some of the key reasons why you should consider starting an online business:

1. **It is inexpensive to start an online business**

Unlike a traditional brick-and-mortar business, starting an online business typically requires less capital and more affordable overhead. With the internet being accessible to anyone, you don't need to rent or buy physical space to do business. In addition, many tools can help you get up and running without needing to invest in expensive software or equipment.

2. **Flexibility of your time**

With an online business, you can set your own hours and work when it's most convenient for you. Working from anywhere gives you the freedom to choose your hours, work on your terms, and still achieve success in your business venture. This is also beneficial for you if you want to balance your professional lives with other commitments such as family or hobbies.

3. **You can start and run your business from home or any location**

If you want to save on costs, starting an online business is a great option for entrepreneurs working from home. This way, you don't have to worry about the overhead of renting or buying physical space.

4. **You can work from any location**

Having the freedom to work from anywhere allows you to take your business with you wherever you go. You can easily move

Is Online Business for You?

your office locations or even work while traveling, as long as you have access to a laptop and an internet connection.

5. Huge income and growth potential

Having an online business gives you the potential to make more money than with a traditional brick-and-mortar store because you can easily sell to anyone wherever they are in the world. Also, if you use the right strategies and techniques, your online business can grow exponentially over time.

6. The business runs 24/7 even when you're sleeping

With an online business, you don't need to worry about closing your doors at the end of a workday. Your online store will stay up and running around the clock so customers can access it whenever necessary. This means that even when you're asleep, your business could be making money.

7. You can reach customers who would never find you offline

The internet is a powerful tool for businesses, allowing them to reach customers who may not have access to their physical store or office space. With an online business, you can utilize digital marketing strategies such as SEO and social media to reach potential customers who may have never found out about your products or services traditionally. You can also use social media and other digital marketing tools to reach potential customers efficiently and effectively. This can open up a whole new world of customers that you may not have been able to reach otherwise.

8. You can access global markets from anywhere with an online business

The internet gives entrepreneurs the ability to sell their products or services globally. With the internet being such a powerful tool, entrepreneurs are no longer limited to conducting business within their local market. With an online business, it is possible to reach customers around the world and capitalize on different trends across multiple regions. This means that you can tap into markets worldwide, increasing your chances of success even further.

9. You can outsource your work

With an online business, you can outsource tasks you don't have the time or expertise to handle. This can help you save time and money on tedious tasks while still allowing you to focus your energy on more important aspects of your business.

10. You can scale up quickly and easily

Since most online business work is done through digital tools and services, you can easily scale up or down your operations depending on the demand for your products or services. This allows you to adjust quickly to changing market conditions and rapidly expand your business as needed.

11. Create long-term financial security

Is Online Business for You?

Having a successful online business can help you establish long-term financial security. With an online store, you can make more money than with traditional methods and have the flexibility to work around your schedule. Additionally, if you use effective strategies and marketing tactics, you can continue to grow your business over time and create sustainable wealth for yourself.

These are just some reasons you should consider starting an online business. With so many opportunities and benefits, it's no wonder why more entrepreneurs are choosing to go digital and start their own businesses. So, if you're looking for a way to make money, create financial freedom, and gain more control over your work-life balance, starting an online business may be the perfect choice for you. Setting up shop online is easier than ever, and there is no shortage of resources available to help you. So, go ahead and take the plunge and start building the future you have always dreamed of!

Different Types of Online Businesses

Not all online business models are the same. Startups today, use a wide range of models. Let's discuss the different types of business models.

1. Manufacturing

Thanks to the internet, businesses can now advertise their products to a broader audience. To cut out the middlemen and sell straight to consumers, several manufacturers have launched their e-commerce websites to sell directly to consumers. Since their pricing and stock levels are entirely under their control, they can offer their consumers better choices and services. This helps to compress and streamline the supply chain. Since wholesaler and distributor margins are not required, the producer can sell the goods at a lower price while still making a larger profit.

2. Advertising

Advertising is a business concept that includes displaying advertising on digital media platforms to earn income. This form of internet business strategy is built on the idea of paying for an advertisement's impressions, clicks, or views.

The advertising approach was influenced by media sites, which have long used this technique. The product is intangible and available for free to users, but advertisements placed throughout the website make it profitable. This model is also available in other variations:

- Portals that rely on high traffic to generate revenue through ad displays (Yahoo, for example),

- Classified websites that sell advertising space and charge subscription fees (like Monster),

- Sites that need users to sign up to view the entire content. The information provided by users is then typically utilized for targeted mailing campaigns, a

Is Online Business for You?

practice extensively used by online newspapers and magazines (such as Les Echos and the Financial Times etc.).

The advertising business model is easy but detracts from the user experience and might work against your website's appeal. Striking a happy medium is key.

3. Intermediary

Online business models that involve a person or organization acting as a go-between in an internet setting are known as "intermediaries." E-commerce, crowdsourcing, and peer-to-peer markets, payment processors are all examples of this business model's numerous guises.

Intermediaries serve as a meeting place for buyers and sellers, facilitating business between them. The cost of their assistance is usually expressed as a percentage of the deal's total or a flat price, often called commission. Sometimes, middlemen may throw in extras like payment processing or advertising services.

A lot of advantages exist for businesses that choose an intermediate internet business strategy. As a bonus, it might make discovering buyers and sellers easier, saving you money when buying and selling. It may also help expand your customer base, opening up new markets that would have been inaccessible.

The intermediate business model allows a consumer-friendly and safe online shopping experience. As the middleman stands between the buyer and the vendor, minimize any potential for fraud or scam.

4. Merchants

To this day, and even before the birth of the internet, merchants have been one of the most common and reliable ways to do business. Retailers that stock up on goods in bulk to resale to customers at a profit are known as merchants, and this can be reproduced online. Online businesses may benefit greatly from this method since it facilitates convenient transactions without needing a physical location.

The advantage of the merchant model is that it enables businesses to provide in-demand goods without manufacturing those products themselves. Instead, retailers buy goods in bulk from producers or wholesalers and resell them to end users online. This, in particular, may greatly benefit small and medium-sized businesses as it reduces their manufacturing and inventory expenses.

This model also allows business owners to adjust to new developments and swiftly satisfy client needs. With the ability to rapidly replenish stock, businesses can always provide consumers with the desired goods. Furthermore, retailers can easily respond to market fluctuations by adjusting pricing, making them an attractive option for businesses trying to boost revenue.

Is Online Business for You?

This business model is an excellent option for businesses that want to remain competitive in the internet market because of their capacity to adapt to new trends swiftly.

5. Subscription

Offering a product or service through client subscription is central to this business strategy. It offers a free version to entice users to pay for premium services. Maybe you've heard the term "freemium." Advertising is commonly utilized in conjunction with this model to improve revenue, as seen in "free access" online games requiring you to pay to access additional gear, levels, time, etc. WeTransfer and Dropbox are two other notable examples: you can use their basic services for free and indefinitely, but you must pay to get their full functionality.

Users may choose to pay for their subscription regularly (every month, every three months, etc.) or depending on how often

they use it (every month, every so many products, etc.).

Customers are drawn to the subscription model because it provides a simple and economical way to access goods and services. Since subscribers pay a predetermined amount on a regular schedule, often monthly, quarterly, or yearly, they don't need to make separate purchases of goods and services in the future.

Many businesses adopt the subscription model because it generates consistent earnings over time. Businesses may use these funds toward ongoing expenses and product development. As subscribers continue to use a company's products or services, brand loyalty may grow with the company's success.

An added benefit of subscriptions is that they allow businesses to amass rich databases of client information. Insights into consumer tastes and preferences enable businesses to serve their clients better. Businesses may use this information to boost customer satisfaction by enhancing customer service.

6. **User group**

User groups are internet businesses that operate on the premise that a group of people can do more together than they can alone. They provide a place for people of similar ideas or interests to share ideas, have conversations, and get answers to their questions. This often includes a wide spectrum of specialists, enthusiasts, and professionals.

User groups, for one thing, are a fantastic venue for commercial

promotion. Businesses may learn more about their target audience and develop lasting connections by participating in community events and activities. Besides helping create new goods and services, research, and customer service, user groups may be used to serve the current clientele better.

Some generate money by organizing events with the data of their customer base. Others profit by selling additional goods and services to the client base. Yet, the viability of such enterprises is determined by the emotional investment made by their target audience in the content. Although if these websites do not earn sufficient profits at first, as they gain popularity, they tend to provide consistent, predictable sources of increasing or continuous cash flow.

7. Cloud-based

A new breed of internet-based business ideas provides on-demand services. The majority of these websites offer applications that clients can utilize without making large expenses in development. Small and medium-sized businesses utilize these apps to ensure they have the same computing capabilities as large corporations. Delivery management systems for logistics companies are common examples of such services. This category also includes hotel management software used by restaurants.

To summarize, not all internet-based businesses are the same. These businesses can be very different from one another. The only thing they have in common is that they all use the internet.

Online Business Myths You Should Discard

From what you've read so far, you can see that starting an online business is easier than launching a typical brick-and-mortar store. Unfortunately, there are several myths about online businesses, some of which you may believe. Let us examine and clarify some of these myths.

1. You can make more money by working less

One of the biggest misconceptions about making money online is the assumption that you can get by with less effort and the same or better results. Get-rich-quick schemes and empty promises of riches spread this misconception. The truth is that you can't cheat your way to success. Work, commitment, and time are essential to succeeding at making money online.

Keep in mind that success is not an instantaneous process. Remember that it may take some time before your online business starts generating significant income. There may be times when you need to put in long hours to create more money. However, this doesn't exclude the possibility that you may someday work less while maintaining a comfortable standard of life.

2. You must budget a significant amount of money for advertising

The misconception that online businesses must spend considerable money on advertising must be debunked. Certainly, marketing can be a powerful tool for any business, whether online or offline, to increase traffic and revenue. However, several alternative strategies may be used to attract customers and boost sales without having to shell out a fortune on marketing. Social media marketing, influencer promotions, and search engine optimization are among them.

Is Online Business for You?

In addition, many no-cost or low-cost web tools are available to help a business get more exposure and revenue. When all is said and done, an online business's fortunes rest on the superiority of its products and the efficiency of its marketing efforts.

3. It is all about passion

It's time to put an end to this persistent falsehood. While enthusiasm is crucial, it is not enough to succeed in business. Starting and growing a successful online business calls for careful planning, plenty of time and effort, and a willingness to constantly educate yourself. A firm grasp of the market, the competitors, and the product or service being offered is also necessary. The ability to think strategically, plan ahead, and carry out your plans are all necessary, in addition to a healthy dose of passion. All are important if you want to achieve your goals.

4. Social media marketing is enough

The success of an online business requires more than just social media marketing. While social media marketing may be effective in reaching a wide audience, it is just one part of a comprehensive digital marketing strategy that includes SEO, content marketing, email marketing, and more.

5. Email marketing is obsolete

Though it has been around for a while, email marketing still has much to offer. It's a great approach to reaching new people and keeping in touch with current clients with little effort and expense. Since email marketing is so specific, you can reach out to many different groups of people and tailor your message to each one individually. It's also easy to monitor and measure. Electronic mail marketing is an effective strategy for establishing rapport with consumers and fostering loyalty.

The truth is, launching a successful online business requires a lot of effort, commitment, and preparation. It's also worth noting that while you're trying to grow your online business, you'll need money from other sources for constant upkeep and to support your business. As an aspiring online business, you'd do well to put these misconceptions to rest if you are serious about being prepared to take on the many obstacles that come with launching and maintaining a successful online business.

Key Takeaways

The best part about starting an online business is that there are plenty of opportunities out there for all sorts of expertise. Whether you're providing services or selling products, whether from your website or through already established platforms – if you're brave enough to take the plunge into entrepreneurship mode, you may find a lot more satisfaction with creating your own income than working for someone else's company.

Is Online Business for You?

However, there are a lot of upsides and downsides to consider when entering an online business. Weigh the pros and cons carefully before you make any decisions that could affect your financial situation in the long run. Ultimately, it is important to find out what is best for you with regard to your own risk tolerance and goals, as well as your budget. With that said, online business opportunities offer flexibility and potential wealth, making them excellent options if you are prepared to take on the challenge.

Starting an online business offers many ways to express who you authentically are as an entrepreneur while making money on your own terms – so why not give it a try?

In the next chapter, we'll review various online business ideas that could spark your interest and give you confidence in moving forward toward success – so stay tuned!

CHAPTER TWO

Online Business Ideas

The internet has opened up many new opportunities for entrepreneurs to create passive income streams and build profitable businesses with little to no upfront investment. From online marketplaces to digital products, the possibilities are endless. However, with so many options available, it can be overwhelming for individuals to choose the right business model. In this chapter, we will explore several lucrative business ideas that you can start at zero cost and provide a guide to help you choose the one to venture into. By the end of this chapter, you will clearly understand the most profitable and sustainable passive income streams and be equipped to take the first steps toward building a successful online business.

10 Most Lucrative Online Businesses

1. Training

Online training has become increasingly popular in recent years. That is because more people seek ways to develop new

Online Business Ideas

skills and knowledge. Online training businesses typically offer courses and programs in various fields, such as business, technology, personal development, and wellness. One of the key benefits of online training is the ability to reach a global audience. That means you can tap into a much larger market than traditional training providers. In addition, you can easily scale an online training business because of its ability to serve hundreds or thousands of students simultaneously. The upfront costs of creating and delivering an online training course can be substantial, but once you create the course, the ongoing costs are relatively low, making it a highly profitable business model.

2. Selling Digital Products

The rise of e-commerce has made it easier than ever for you to sell digital products online. Digital products can include eBooks, online courses, software, music, and many other types of digital content. One of the benefits of selling digital products is the ability to create and distribute the products at a low cost, which means that profit margins can be very high. Digital products can also be highly scalable, as they can be downloaded and delivered instantly to customers worldwide. With the right marketing strategy, you can build a loyal following of customers and generate significant revenue from digital product sales.

3. Blogging

Blogging has become a popular way for people to share their thoughts and experiences online, and it can also be a highly profitable business model. Successful bloggers can generate revenue from various sources, including advertising, affiliate marketing, and sponsored content. One of the key benefits of blogging is the ability to build a loyal audience of readers who are interested in the content you're producing. You can leverage this audience to generate revenue from advertising or affiliate marketing, as businesses are often willing to pay for access to a highly engaged audience. While building a successful blog can take time and effort, the potential rewards can be amazing.

4. Freelancing

The rise of remote work has created a growing demand for freelance writers and other freelancers, such as graphic designers, web developers, and social media managers. Freelancers can work with clients all over the world. The flexibility of the work can be highly appealing to many individuals. The key to success in freelancing is to build a strong reputation and a solid network of clients. By delivering high-quality projects and providing excellent customer service, you can build a loyal client base that can generate a steady income stream over time.

5. Amazon FBA

Amazon FBA (Fulfillment by Amazon) is a business model that allows you to sell physical products on Amazon by taking advantage of the company's vast distribution network. With Amazon FBA, you can send your products to Amazon's fulfillment centers, where the company will handle all the logistics of picking, storing, and shipping the product once a customer places an order, and it provides customer service. This model can be highly profitable since it allows you to take advantage of Amazon's massive customer base and established reputation. The key to success in Amazon FBA is identifying high-demand products and creating a strong brand that can stand out in a crowded marketplace.

6. **Vlogging – Start a Niche YouTube Channel**

YouTube has become a dominant force in online video, with over two billion monthly active users. Many entrepreneurs, YouTubers as they are proudly called, have found success by building YouTube channels around a specific niche, such as gaming, beauty, cooking, or travel. These channels can generate revenue from advertising, sponsorships, and product sales. The key to success on YouTube is creating high-quality, engaging content that appeals to a specific audience and consistently promoting the channel to grow the audience over time.

7. **Amazon Affiliate Website**

Amazon has one of the largest affiliate marketing programs in the world, and many entrepreneurs have built successful businesses by creating websites that promote Amazon products. Amazon affiliate websites typically feature product reviews, buying guides, and other content that helps customers make informed purchasing decisions. You earn a commission on any products sold through your affiliate links. The key to success in this business model is to build a website that provides value to customers and promotes it to generate traffic and sales effectively.

8. Review blog

A review blog is a website that provides product reviews in a

specific niche. Many consumers rely on reviews to make purchasing decisions, so there is a strong demand for high-quality, unbiased reviews. Review bloggers can generate revenue from advertising, sponsorships, and affiliate marketing. To be successful, you have to provide honest and detailed reviews that provide value to readers and effectively promote the blog to generate traffic and revenue.

9. Drop-shipping

Drop-shipping is another profitable online business model that has recently gained popularity. It involves selling products online without holding any inventory or handling the shipping process. With drop shipping, you work with a supplier or manufacturer to fulfill orders on behalf of the customer. When a customer orders on your online store, the supplier will help you package and ship the product directly to the customer.

One of the main advantages of drop shipping is that it requires little to no upfront investment. There is no need to purchase inventory or pay for storage space, which reduces the risk and startup costs for you. In addition, drop-shipping allows for greater flexibility and scalability, as you can easily add or remove products from your website without any physical constraints.

To succeed in drop-shipping, you need to have a deep understanding of your target market and be able to market your products effectively. You need to identify profitable niches and products with high demand and low competition. In addition, you need to build a strong brand and customer base by providing excellent customer service, offering competitive

pricing, and delivering high-quality products.

10. Domain Investing and Website Flipping

Domain investing and website flipping involve buying and selling domains and websites for a profit. Domain investors purchase domain names they believe have high value and then sell them for a profit. Website flippers purchase websites, improve them, and then sell them for a higher price. The key to success in this business model is to effectively identify undervalued domains and websites and market them to potential buyers.

The internet has created vast opportunities to start and grow profitable online businesses. The key to success in any of these lucrative online businesses is to identify the right market, create high-quality products or services, and develop a strong marketing strategy to reach potential customers. These businesses require time, effort, and dedication to build. But with the right approach, they can be a great source of income and offer you great flexibility and freedom if you're willing to work.

10 Online Businesses You Can Start with No Money

In recent years, the growth of the internet has created many opportunities for people to start their businesses with little to no money. You can start with a computer and an internet connection with numerous online business ideas. You can start any of these businesses as a side hustle or grow them into full-time businesses. Many of the businesses previously mentioned will also fall into this category.

1. **Affiliate marketing**

Affiliate marketing is a great online business model that allows you to earn a commission by promoting products or services. You can join affiliate programs like Click Bank, Warrior Plus, JVZoo, and Amazon Associates and select and promote products through blogs, social media, or email marketing.

2. **Running a blog**

Blogging is an excellent way to create content and generate traffic to a website. You can start a blog for free using platforms like WordPress and Blogger. You can monetize your blog through advertising, affiliate marketing, and product sales.

Online Business Ideas

3. Becoming a community manager

Community managers manage and engage with a company's social media and online communities. You can do this remotely. Many companies are willing to hire community managers on a freelance basis.

4. Offering translation services

If you're bilingual, offering translation services can be a lucrative business. You can work as a freelance translator with clients all over the world. You can offer your services on platforms like Upwork and Fiverr.

5. Offering SEO services

Search engine optimization (SEO) is essential to digital marketing, and many businesses are willing to pay for SEO services. You can learn SEO strategies and offer your services to clients looking to improve their search engine rankings.

6. Data entry

Data entry is a straightforward online business that involves entering data into a computer system. You can do this remotely, and many companies are willing to hire data entry freelancers to help them enter data online.

7. Cooking vlog

If you love to cook, you can start a cooking vlog and share your recipes and cooking tips with your audience. You can monetize your content through advertising, sponsorships, and product sales.

8. Providing content services

Content services include writing, editing, proofreading, etc. You can offer these services on platforms like Upwork and Fiverr.

9. Web design

Web design is an in-demand skill, and many businesses are willing to pay top dollar for web design services. Individuals with web design skills can offer their services on platforms like Upwork and Fiverr.

10. Creating a podcast

Podcasting is a great way to share your knowledge and build an audience. You can create podcasts for free on platforms like Zencastr and Riverside FM and monetize your content through sponsorships, advertising, and selling their products.

Many online business ideas can be started with no money. With determination and hard work, you can start your online business and turn it into a successful venture. The key to success is identifying a profitable niche, building a strong brand, and providing high-quality products or services.

50 Other Online Business Ideas

Online Business Ideas

There is no shortage of ideas when starting an online business. Here is more option: a list of 50 great internet business ideas that could help you on your journey toward success.

1. **Mobile apps development**

Mobile app development is a highly sought-after skill, and developing mobile applications may be a successful business venture. With the growing popularity of smartphones, more organizations and people are attempting to create mobile applications to reach their target audience. You can provide mobile app development services to companies, entrepreneurs, or anyone who wants to build an app. Begin by developing your portfolio and marketing your skills on social media and

freelancing networks.

2. **Earn from online survey sites**

For people with free time and a desire to earn some extra money, online survey sites may be a terrific source of income. Begin by registering with reliable survey sites and completing surveys for money. You can also earn extra by referring friends via their referral program. This business involves little capital and allows you to work from anywhere, making it a perfect alternative if you wish to earn money online.

3. **Instagram consulting**

Instagram is one of the world's biggest social media sites, with over one billion monthly active users. Companies and individuals continuously seek new strategies to enhance their

Instagram following and engagement. Account administration, content development, influencer marketing, and analytics are all services that you could provide as an Instagram consultant. Start by creating your own Instagram account, establishing your reputation, and marketing your services to prospective clients.

4. **Digital marketing agency**

Digital marketing has become integral to online businesses and product promotion. Search engine optimization (SEO), social media management, email marketing, content marketing, and pay-per-click (PPC) advertising are all services that a digital marketing firm may provide. You can start by assembling a team of professionals and marketing your services to small businesses, entrepreneurs, and anyone looking to improve their

online presence.

5. **Sell handmade crafts online**

If you have a gift for crafting unique items, you may convert it into a lucrative business. You can sell your handmade products on websites like Etsy, Amazon, or your own e-commerce business. You may also improve your earnings by providing specialized services, such as producing customized or personalized items.

6. **Graphic design service**

Online Business Ideas

Graphic design is an important part of corporate branding and marketing. You can provide small companies and entrepreneurs with graphic design services, such as logo creation, branding, site design, and social media design. Start by developing your portfolio and marketing your skills on freelancing marketplaces or social media.

7. Make videos/video editing service

As video content becomes more popular, businesses seek ways to generate exciting and engaging content. You can provide services such as animation, explainer, and short video creation as a video content creator. Start by developing your portfolio and marketing your skills on social media and freelancing networks.

8. Internet marketing consulting

Internet marketing consulting is all about providing businesses

with the latest strategies and tactics they need to succeed. A consultant will be able to analyze the current landscape of digital marketing, identify any potential opportunities, create a strategic plan, and execute campaigns that will help businesses reach their goals.

9. IT security consulting

Cybersecurity is becoming a more critical component of corporate operations. As an IT security consultant, you can provide services such as cybersecurity risk assessments, network security, and data protection. Start by establishing your reputation and marketing your services to small firms and entrepreneurs.

10. Virtual assistant

Virtual assistants offer administrative assistance to firms and entrepreneurs remotely. As a virtual assistant, you can provide email management, appointment scheduling, social media management, and customer support. Start by establishing a reputation and publicizing your skills on freelancing platforms and social media.

11. Online grocery delivery

You may enter this developing market by starting your own online grocery delivery business. You may collaborate with local grocery retailers to provide online ordering and delivery services.

12. Sell handbags online

You can start an online business selling handbags with a website and social media accounts. Purchasing an inventory of handbags needs some investment, but it may be beneficial as the business grows.

13. Online scholarship directory

This is a fantastic online business. You just need to create a directory of scholarship options for students. The website may

Online Business Ideas

generate revenue via advertising and affiliate programs. Students may use the website for free, while institutions or scholarship providers can advertise for a fee.

14. Online juror

As an online juror, you may participate in simulated trials, which assist attorneys in preparing for real court cases. This online business needs a decent internet connection and may pay anywhere between $10 and $60 for each case.

15. Online outsourcing

This type of online business involves providing services to businesses or people that want certain tasks completed, such as data entry, social media management, content authoring, and so on. You may create a website or join platforms such as Upwork or Fiverr to get customers.

16. Auction selling

This business involves purchasing products at auctions and

selling them at a higher price online on eBay, Amazon Auction, or Craigslist.

17. Make Funny Videos

You can create comedy videos and upload them to YouTube or other social media sites. You can earn advertising revenue on them if any of the videos go viral and garner many views.

18. Build an online music community

You may start an online music community where members can discuss their favorite music, attend virtual concerts, and exchange playlists. Advertising, affiliate marketing, and membership fees are all ways you can profit from this business.

19. Online dancing club

This online business aims to create a virtual dance club where individuals may learn and practice dancing with others. You can earn from this business by charging a membership fee or for individual classes.

20. Start an online music school

You can launch an online music school to provide virtual music instruction. This online business requires some initial investment in equipment and promotion, but it has the potential to be lucrative.

21. Resell PLR products

Private Label Rights (PLR) products are digital products with

resell rights. You simply buy them from the owner and resell them under your brand name. This online business involves an initial investment but can be profitable since the items can be resold.

22. Make money from Facebook

Online Business Ideas

You can make a Facebook page, create engaging video content, and earn money through advertising. To succeed here, you must create content that is appealing to a certain audience and build a huge following.

23. Social media influencer

You can make money through sponsored posts and advertising as a social media influencer. You need to build a huge following and also create appealing content.

24. Selling photographs online

You can sell images online by creating a website for your photos or joining networks such as Shutterstock or iStock. This online business requires a decent camera and some photography skills.

25. Internet Café

An internet cafe is a physical venue where individuals may use computers and access the internet. It is an online business involving capital investment in equipment and infrastructure, but it can be successful.

26. Selling things on eBay

This is another online business opportunity you could try out. It requires you to create an eBay account and list items you want to sell. Selling items at a higher price than the cost price allows you to make a profit.

27. Live streaming

Create a live streaming channel on sites like YouTube and make money from advertising, sponsorships, and contributions. You will need to create captivating content as well as grow a huge following.

28. Offer voice-over services

You may provide voice-over services for videos, advertisements, and audiobooks. This online business requires a decent microphone and some voice-acting abilities.

29. Online magazine

Starting an online magazine and earning money through advertising, subscriptions, and sponsorships is possible. You will need editorial skills.

30. Artist

You could be a musician, an artist, a writer, or just a creative person. You can make money no matter what type of creative skills you have. The best part is that you can run this business from home.

31. Internet Security

Create and market internet security software if you are a software developer or have a strong interest in it. This business requires competence in cybersecurity and marketing.

Online Business Ideas

32. Proofreading

Provide proofreading services to individuals or businesses that need their writing double-checked for errors. This online business requires you to have exceptional language abilities and proofreading expertise.

33. Provide virtual fitness training

You can provide virtual fitness training by creating a website or using platforms like Zoom. To attract customers, this online business needs experience in fitness instruction and marketing.

34. Create mobile applications for kids

You can create mobile apps for kids and make money from app sales and advertising income. You have to be proficient in app development and have skills in building applications for children.

35. Make and sell Homemade goods

One may start an internet company by making and selling handcrafted products such as jewelry, ceramics, or knitwear on platforms such as Etsy. To gain clients, solid craft skills and marketing are required.

36. Print-on-demand T-shirts

You can even launch your own business using print-on-demand services such as Redbubble or Society6. You upload your own designs, which are then printed on items such as T-shirts and mugs.

37. Group buying

You can start a group buying service where consumers can enjoy discounts on items or services by buying them in bulk. Group buying is an excellent way for buyers to reduce costs and for businesses to increase sales.

38. On-demand app creator

You may create on-demand applications like Uber or Airbnb and earn money from app sales and commissions. You must have some experience in app development and marketing to attract clients.

39. Offer chatbot solutions

Provide chatbot solutions to businesses that want automated customer service. You need expertise in chatbot creation and marketing.

40. Food ordering system

You can make money online by developing a food ordering system for restaurants or cafés. This could work for you if you are proficient in web development, marketing, and business

management.

41. Video Editing

Online Business Ideas

Offer video editing services to people or businesses that want video content editing and smile to the bank. The basic requirements are experience with video editing software and marketing.

42. Interior design consultant

Can you provide interior design consulting services to individuals or businesses? If yes, you can make money online by offering that service. The requirements are knowledge of interior design, marketing, and business operations.

43. Skype coaching

Have you acquired any skills that you'd want to share with others? If yes, then Skype coaching could be an opportunity for you. Generally, you connect to Skype and support your coaching clients. This could take the shape of daily, weekly, or monthly meetings. There are Skype coaches for almost anything – life coaches, health coaches, dating coaches, and so on.

44. Stock management system

A stock management system enables merchants to monitor and manage their inventory in real-time. It can assist in optimizing the supply chain and lowering the expenses of selling items.

45. Create WordPress themes

Creating WordPress themes as an online business is a great approach to making passive income since once the theme is released, you can profit from recurrent purchases. Moreover, it offers a one-of-a-kind chance to reach a worldwide audience and make a significant profit.

46. Data analytics start-up

Data analysis businesses provide customers with full data analysis services such as data collecting, modeling, and visualization to assist them in making informed decisions. These services may be provided via a simple web platform that enables clients to quickly and simply access and see their data.

47. Technical writing

You can make money by delivering technical writing services to people or businesses who want documentation for their goods or services. Getting customers requires competence in technical writing and marketing.

48. Creating listings or ads

You can build an online business by creating listings or advertising for people or businesses needing assistance promoting their goods or services. You can learn how to run ad campaigns on various platforms like Facebook and Google.

49. Paid private Facebook group

It provides a platform for you to distribute your content, allows your community members to connect, enables you to restrict access to qualified members, and allows you to moderate and control the group.

50. Self-Publish eBooks

If you want to write a book, self-publishing allows you to do everything on your own. You can also make eBooks so users can download your content rather than purchasing a physical copy.

Generally, the Internet is brimming with money-making opportunities – one after the other. The best part is that you can launch some of these business ideas on other platforms if you don't have much money to launch your website.

Profitable Niches in the Online Business

You may have the buzzword "Niche" that has dominated the online space. Before I reveal some profitable internet business you can venture into, let's properly understand the word "Niche".

What is a niche?

A niche market is a market segment with its own particular needs and wants. It's essentially a smaller, more focused version of an overall market. Niche markets can be found in all industries. They offer unique opportunities to capitalize on specific needs not being served by mainstream competition.

Niche markets are appealing because they allow businesses to specialize, stand out from the competition, and focus their resources on a target audience. This allows them to offer more specialized products and services to their customers. By focusing on a particular market segment, you can start targeting more specific customer needs and capitalize on those opportunities.

One you need to know is that niche markets aren't necessarily small. While they may have fewer overall customers than a larger market, they can still be quite profitable if you can deliver what they need. For example, if you were selling a product specifically geared towards dog owners with large breeds, your niche might not be too large but could still offer significant sales potential.

Niche markets are attractive for businesses because they can build stronger relationships with their target customers and more easily assess what new products or services they should add to their offerings. Overall, niches allow entrepreneurs to create unique value and capitalize on opportunities that larger markets may overlook.

With the right strategy, you can succeed by targeting niche markets with high potential and strong customer loyalty. By focusing your resources on a specific market segment, you can create something special and unique that your customers will appreciate. So, if you're looking for a way to stand out and make an impact, exploring niche markets is definitely worth considering.

Online Business Ideas

Now it's clear why finding a niche for your online business is important. But if you think that the task is too daunting or don't know where to begin, don't worry. I've got you covered with some of the best niches out there. So get ready, and let's dive into finding just the right fit for your success story.

Weight Loss and fitness

This will always be a profitable niche business, and anyone can have a piece of the pie, or should I say apple. People have been obsessed with getting in shape and losing weight for centuries. They're always on the lookout for the next workout program, fad diet, or magic pill to help them achieve their goals, and that's where you come in. You can even niche down to nutrition, exercise, dieting, and weight loss or control.

Make money online

This niche is dedicated to teaching people how to make money online. It may include things like blogging, affiliate marketing, producing digital items, and providing online services. You can create your own digital in this niche with the knowledge and experience or sell other people's products via affiliate marketing. With people looking for work-from-home opportunities, this niche will always be profitable.

Dating and relationships

Whether someone is interested in online dating or looking for love ... Several goods in the dating and relationships category are available to assist anyone single, dating, or who is in a relationship but is having trouble and wants to find a solution to reignite the fire. People always seek guidance in this area because it's one of life's necessities and one of the most challenging.

Promoting dating websites is one of the potential businesses here; several companies pay commissions to marketers who refer them to new sign-ups. Also, you might advertise "pick up" manuals, books on enhancing communication and relationships, and more.

There are numerous options to niche down even further. There are different ways to approach dating, including dating for straight couples, dating for gay couples, dating and relationships for specific religious groups, etc.

Dating and relationships will always be a sizable niche market with a lot of profit potential, whether for singles, couples, divorcees, etc.

Pets

Have you ever seen a pet owner? They love their pets. There are over 180 million dogs and cats in the United States alone. A huge market in this niche is dog training. People want to potty train their new puppies as soon as possible. Many also want to train older dogs for obedience, security, and even tricks. If you are passionate about training pets, you may produce your own information products, such as eBooks. You

Online Business Ideas

may just work as an affiliate and sell other people's books and courses.

The truth is that many pet owners treat their animals well and

spend more on them than they do on themselves, and this niche market is only expanding each year.

Self-improvement

This is a huge niche online and is also referred to as self-help. Books, videos, online training, coaching, and courses and programs exist. Self-improvement products are available for everyone who wishes to improve their self-worth, experience career success, boost their confidence, set and achieve goals, or overcome challenges.

Gadgets and Technology

It doesn't matter if it's a tablet or smartphone, computer speakers, mp3 players, smart home devices, thumb drives, cellphone cases, or earphones; people love accessories and gadgets. Everyone desires the latest technology. In a few different ways, you can profit from that.

Selling the products through an online retailer like Amazon as an affiliate would be the easiest. Alternatively, you could import products using a website like Alibaba.com or Aliexpress.com, which connects you to foreign manufacturers and wholesalers.

You have to focus on marketing once you have the products. One strategy is to make money blogging, highlighting all the newest products and technology. Another option is to run a review website where you provide opinions on various goods within a given category. Of course, a link to purchase each product includes your affiliate link.

Real Estate

The real estate sector is another billion-dollar industry, with several agents building niche websites, controlling particular markets, and reaping yearly profits. This would be ideal for you if you are interested in the real estate industry. This niche focuses on delivering real estate-related information, goods, and services. It may include sub-niches like buying and selling real estate, investing in real estate, and home repair.

Personal Finance

When it comes to the personal finance niche, there are not enough needs for things like credit scores, mortgage refinancing, debt relief, personal loans, etc. People need assistance managing their finances or obtaining the funds required for important expenditures.

Perhaps, they are in debt and require help reducing it or obtaining a cheaper interest rate. Maybe they have to file for bankruptcy and need assistance with the procedure. In extreme circumstances, it's possible that they received the dreaded IRS letter informing them that they owe past taxes.

Online Business Ideas

In any event, you won't be providing legal assistance. But, you can link potential customers with financial experts, work as an affiliate to market information products, or provide affiliate-only services for products like credit monitoring. There are numerous options in this huge niche. You can also help people in resolving these problems and enhance their financial status by creating e-learning and educational products.

Babies

As long as humans are on the planet, there will be a demand for baby products. You can launch a drop-shipping store and sell any products you like. So, what kind of products should you pick? Clothing, cosmetics, toys, or other items. You must research to determine what your business can provide that other drop-shipping businesses in this niche cannot.

There are other things to consider in this niche as well. Parents sometimes want to unwind while their adorable newborns sleep in their beds. Parents can monitor their baby's behavior with the use of baby monitors. Some baby monitors are audio-only devices, while others have a built-in camera that allows parents to watch their baby through a mobile app. Almost all parents will want a baby monitor because they serve a useful purpose.

Gaming

You would be surprised to know there are 2.5 billion gamers worldwide and that the gaming market will be valued at about $256 billion by 2025. These data unequivocally prove that it is among the top niches to focus on if you seek a lucrative blogging niche. Go for it if you have any interest in and enjoy playing video games. Play games and make money while encouraging others to play.

Travel

Most people, including employees, businesspeople, and students, all desire to travel. The majority of people even have global travel dreams. As a result, the traveling niche is now a $1 billion industry. You can get your own share of the money in this industry. Some sub-niche ideas include travel advice, holiday planning, and vacation locations.

A smart strategy to launch your internet business is to focus on creating a business in a popular niche. No need for guesswork. They are products that people want and are built on innate human needs and desires that will always exist. With the information on profitable niches at your disposal, your market research will start much faster, which means you could start earning money online much sooner than you had anticipated.

Choosing the Best Online Business for You

Having the right idea when deciding to launch an online business is necessary, but it's more important to stay away from bad ones. No matter how wonderful the business idea

Online Business Ideas

may seem, it will fail without an adequate plan, patience, and foresight. Setting up an online business requires a significant investment of time, energy, and even cash in some cases.

It demands dedication. A determination to continue no matter what happens. There must be patience. Before reaching its full potential, your business must take baby steps. If you've ever experienced the exciting anxiety of launching your own business, you must know that success doesn't happen overnight. You must take it seriously and understand what is needed to properly take care of it to build a business that can withstand

the test of time.

Whatever your business will be – whether you've already decided or are still considering it – remember that any effort you presently make will determine your future reward. Having said all this, make sure you start the right online business if you're actually ready to jump in and do it. Pick the one that best fits your needs and interests. Don't put all of your attention on the money; instead, consider your interests and personality.

The following are the top guidelines for selecting an online business venture.

1. **Determine your start-up investment**

Every business needs to make initial time and financial investments. Asking yourself this honest question will help you determine how much you will invest. Figure out how much you can invest in your business without sacrificing your responsibilities and basic needs. Starting little is better than not starting at all, so make the smallest investments first and get things going. For a business to flourish, it must first start. Reinvest your early profits to foster your business growth.

2. What kind of support/training is available?

New business owners can learn how to handle the ups and downs through training. They can also improve their overall business skills with the right support. That you are seeking support or training is not a sign that you can't manage your business. It's an indication that you are prepared to utilize every resource and advantage at your disposal to help your business succeed.

3. Could Compensation Be Delayed?

At the end of the day, business is still about making money. Consider whether you want to wait to reap the rewards of your efforts or only want a quick financial gain. While starting your venture, you have to set attainable goals. It might not be the best time to launch a business if your budget prevents you from waiting to see measurable profits.

4. Do you have confidence in your business?

Do you actually love what you're selling – if you launched a product-based business? Nobody else will believe in your product if you don't. It is the same for service-based businesses. Do you trust the services your business is offering? Do you feel that your offer will be helpful to others?

You should be able to choose the best idea for you now that we have established the four golden rules for selecting the ideal online business concept.

Understanding Online Business Models

Online business models refer to businesses' specific strategies to sell products or services online. Here, we will discuss the most common online business models and their features.

B2C (Business-to-Consumer)

This business strategy entails marketing and selling goods or services to end users individually. Companies like Amazon and Zappos are great examples of businesses that use this model. A web-based storefront, an online shopping cart, and an integrated payment gateway are essential components of this model.

B2B (Business-to-Business)

This model involves marketing your goods or services to other companies in the market. Alibaba and Grainger are two companies that are examples of businesses using this strategy. A company portal, an automated quotation request system, and an automated billing system are all integral components of this model.

C2C (Consumer-to-Consumer)

In this business model, people offer their products or services to other individuals through an online marketplace. eBay and Etsy are two companies that use this business strategy. A product listing, a user profile, and a payment mechanism are some of the most important aspects of this model.

B2B2C (Business-to-Business-to-Consumer)

Under this model, one company sells its goods or services to another, which markets and sells those goods or services to end users. Alibaba and eBay are only two examples of firms that use this business model. A product catalog, a payment mechanism,

and an online business site are some of the essential components of this model.

B2G (Business-to-Government)

This business strategy depends on winning government contract bids. A government agency will normally post a proposal request (RFP), and e-commerce businesses must submit bids for these projects.

C2B (Consumer-to-Business)

Online Business Ideas

In this business model, customers sell their goods or services directly to other companies. Fiverr and Upwork are two examples of businesses that use this business model. A user profile, a directory of available services, and a payment mechanism are all integral components of this model.

D2C (Direct-to-Consumer)

Under this business model, manufacturers sell products directly to users without going through any middlemen, such as retail stores. Companies like Warby Parker and Casper are good examples of businesses that use this approach. A web-based storefront, an online shopping cart, and an integrated payment gateway are essential components of this model.

It is important to remember that some of these models are formed to provide a more intricate online shopping environment. For instance, a corporation may utilize a B2B2C model to sell its goods to another business, which would then use a B2C model to sell those items directly to end users (consumers). When selecting a business model, it is essential to consider the product or service you want to sell, the demographics of your ideal customers, and the approach you will use to advertise it.

Tips for Choosing a Successful Online Business

Starting an online business can be a great way to make money and launch your career. But with so many options, it can be difficult to choose the right one. To help you make an informed decision, here are some tips for selecting a successful online business that fits your skills and goals.

1. Research the industry

Before you choose a particular online business, you must research the industry and related markets or niches. This will give you a better understanding of its dynamics, challenges, opportunities, and growth potential. Try to get an up-close view with customers or industry professionals; this way, you can gain insights into how to tailor your business model for success.

2. Evaluate potential risks and rewards

Before jumping in, you have to assess the potential risks and rewards. Consider how much effort and money you'll need to invest, your expected return on that investment, and how long it may take to get there. Also, consider any legal requirements that come with launching an online business.

3. Understand legal requirements

Every online business has its legal requirements, so it's important to understand all the regulations and laws affecting your industry. Research any licenses or permits you may need and any taxes you'll have to pay.

4. Create a business plan

Online Business Ideas

Once you've evaluated all the risks and rewards, it's time to create a business plan. This document should include a detailed description of your business, a short- and long-term strategy for growth, and an analysis of the competition.

5. Launch your business

The final step is to launch your online business. Take all the steps necessary to set it up properly, including registering with the government, creating a website, and marketing your business.

By following these tips, you can ensure that you choose the right online business for your skills and goals. With a bit of effort and research, launching an online business can be a great way to make money and jumpstart your career.

Successful Online Businesses You Can Learn From

The success of a new online business may be greatly improved

by learning from established practices. Learning from brands that have excelled in their businesses is important since they provide significant insight into how to manage an online business effectively.

Successful businesses have a strong brand identity, serve a niche market, and have a well-established online presence.

Analyzing the techniques of successful companies may assist you in determining what works and what does not. Learning from the successes and failures of others may save you time and money, help you avoid common pitfalls, and set yourself up for success.

FUGOO

This company makes durable Bluetooth speakers intended for use on the move. They encountered difficulties while joining an already congested market with established competitors. With a limited launch window, FUGOO focused on preparing for the Consumer Electronics Show and launching their product through a conversion-friendly online buying experience and targeted marketing campaigns. Its website included direct-product comparisons that emphasized FUGOO's strong qualities compared to other manufacturers. As a result, the company had a successful launch, with a 300% increase in sales year over year and top organic search placement.

Some of the lessons you can learn from FUGOO include:

- Concentrate on a limited launch window and prepare for a significant event to premiere the product or service.

- Provide a conversion-friendly online shopping experience

  to entice people to buy.

Online Business Ideas

- Develop highly focused marketing campaigns to reach prospective buyers efficiently.

- Through direct comparisons to your competitors, highlight your product or service's unique characteristics and advantages.

- Invest in search engine optimization (SEO) to rank high in organic search results.

Black Milk Clothing

James Lillis founded Black Milk Clothing, a bespoke pants business. With limited marketing budgets, Lillis had to find other methods to promote his product, which has now developed into a multimillion-dollar enterprise with over 150 workers.

Black Milk Clothing's community-building activities have been a big component of its success. The firm has formed tribe-like groups with brand ambassadors, each with its own Facebook group for each location where it sells its product. This method, which includes over 80 distinct Facebook groups, provides more customized connections and encourages people to chat about the brand even when it is not being pushed.

Lessons to learn from Black Milk Apparel include:

- Community-building activities may be a powerful strategy to expand your company and establish brand loyalty.

- Creating distinct social media communities may help enhance engagement and encourage brand discussions.

- Customized client involvement may help in developing a strong customer connection.

- Encouraging user-generated content and consumer reviews may help your business gain trust and reputation.

- Establishing a feeling of belonging or community around your brand may help it become ingrained in your consumers' lives.

Common Projects

Common Projects is a shoe brand that began in 2004, emphasizing modest men's footwear. The firm expanded slowly and steadily without significant initial investment, remaining focused on its core product rather than extending out to provide too many items, which would overwhelm its tiny operations. It took several years for Common Projects to introduce women's shoes to their collection.

Collaborations with designers and influencers helped Common Projects flourish by allowing them to reach a bigger market and expose many new clients to the quality and styles of their shoes.

Lessons you can learn from Common Projects include:

Online Business Ideas

- Keeping a focus on your main product and resisting the need to diversify too rapidly.

- Slowly and methodically expanding your business without depending on major investments or incurring excessive debt.

- Working with designers and influencers to reach a broader audience and acquire new consumers.

- Creating a reputation for excellence and distinctive design that distinguishes your brand from the competition.

- Maintaining your brand's identity when you extend your product offerings or enter new markets.

Seismic Audio

Seismic Audio is a firm founded on eBay in 2004 by CEO Steve Acree. He increased the company's sales to more than $120,000 annually by 2009, reaching $10 million annually in 2015. Acree maintained his company for years on eBay before moving into Amazon and other internet channels in 2007.

You can learn the following lessons from Seismic Audio:

- Start small and concentrate on creating a strong foundation for your business.

- Create a scalable business model that can adapt to market changes.

- Take note of consumer feedback and use it to enhance your products and services.

- Invest in your brand to establish a reputation for quality and value.

- Be ready to take reasonable chances and adjust to market developments but avoid taking unnecessary risks that might hurt your business.

Finch Goods

This is an online retailer of high-quality, sustainable men's grooming products. Finch Goods emphasizes customer experience and retention strategies to drive traffic and improve conversion rates. Here are some key online businesses lessons that you can learn from Finch Goods:

- Consistently drive traffic to your website.

- Develop a strategic marketing plan and funnel.

- Utilize upsell offers during checkout to improve average order value.

- Capture customers' email addresses with a newsletter opt-in popup.

- Use abandoned cart emails for remarketing to customers.

- Transform customers into brand ambassadors with referral offers.

Online Business Ideas

- Utilize exit-intent popups with special offers to encourage purchases.

- Retarget customers with Facebook pixels and AdWords.

- Offer customer loyalty programs to improve returning customer rates.

- Regularly send newsletter emails with product updates and offers.

Amazon

You can learn a lot from Amazon, a leader in the e-commerce industry. Amazon is a global technology company known for its e-commerce, digital streaming, and cloud computing services. They are well-known for their large product offerings, quick delivery, and customized shopping experience.

Here are some lessons you can learn from Amazon:

- Page load time is important for online sales. Page performance optimization should be done to improve user experience and boost revenue.

- The average order value may be greatly increased by personalizing the buying experience.

- Search bar optimization is important. Displaying popular products and categories in the search bar may enhance the user experience.

- Customers can use reviews to make informed purchase decisions. Product reviews and feedback should be prioritized.

- Offering similar products and bundling them together can boost average order value.

- Businesses need to test various plans and techniques. To improve performance and boost revenue, you have to experiment.

Diamond Candles

This company sells scented candles with a unique twist: each candle contains a ring hidden inside the wax. When customers light the candle and it burns down, they eventually uncover a ring that can be worn. The company initially struggled with marketing due to budget constraints. But it found success by leveraging user-generated content on social media to gain brand exposure and acquire a large following without spending money on advertising.

You can learn the following lessons from Diamond Candles:

- Leverage user-generated content for marketing and brand awareness

- Encourage customers to share pictures of their experiences with your product on social media

- Use striking imagery to make your posts more appealing

Online Business Ideas

- Focus on building a strong following on social media platforms

- Creatively differentiate your product to stand out in a crowded market.

Hello Matcha

Shopify's product team established this Matcha green tea product line. To identify a product based on consumer trends, the team thoroughly studied the present e-commerce industry. With a limited budget and schedule, they created a premium brand and product packaging, which they promoted using a content-focused approach.

Lessons you can learn from Hello Matcha include:

- To find a product based on customer trends, do a comprehensive study on the existing e-commerce industry.

- Develop a high-quality brand and product packaging to make your product stand out from the competition.

- To increase interest in your product, utilize a content-focused marketing approach.

- Set the project's spending limit and period to ensure it remains on track and under budget.

- Focus on generating revenue early in the product launch cycle to gain momentum and develop a strong market presence.

The online business world has become incredibly large, with many different options and ways to make money. We have just discussed some of the principles and strategies that successful online businesses employ to be successful, and you should consider applying what you've learned to your own endeavor. After all, success is not always handed to us on a silver platter; we must take the time and effort to learn and understand how other businesses succeed in theirs.

Key Takeaways

When you're ready to start an online business, it's important to weigh your options carefully. There are many different types of businesses out there, and you'll want to ensure that the one you choose fits your skill set and interests.

Now that you understand various online businesses you can possibly start, it's time to carve out your own lane in this ever-evolving industry. In the next chapter, you will learn how to develop an entrepreneurial mindset and implement strategies that help bring your vision to fruition. The possibilities are endless when it comes to taking control of your financial destiny and creating a profitable business using only the power of the internet. Your success depends on you.

Online Business Ideas

CHAPTER THREE

Cultivating an Entrepreneurial Mindset

The entrepreneurial mindset combines attitudes and skills that allow you to see opportunities, take calculated risks, and provide value to the marketplace. It entails thinking creatively, innovating, adapting to change, and acting in the face of uncertainty. In today's fast-paced and ever-changing business environment, cultivating an entrepreneurial attitude is critical for success.

The entrepreneurial attitude is particularly vital when it comes to online businesses. Online businesses operate in a fiercely competitive and dynamic market, where developments happen fast, and customer requirements and tastes may fluctuate. To thrive in an online business, you must be creative, dynamic, and quick to adjust to industry trends.

Some significant features of the entrepreneurial attitude that relate to online businesses are as follows:

- **Recognizing opportunities:** you must be able to discover new possibilities and respond swiftly to market developments. This entails being current with industry developments, tracking client needs and preferences, and being proactive in searching out new growth potentials.

- **Positive thinking:** you must be optimistic about remaining motivated and conquering problems. Focusing on solutions rather than problems is important, and building a positive mindset encourages creativity and innovation.

- **Goal-oriented mindset:** you have to strive to establish specific, quantifiable goals and work hard to attain them. You need to prioritize your time and resources and regularly analyze your progress toward your objectives, making modifications as needed.

- **Resilience to failure:** failure is an inevitable part of the entrepreneurial journey, so you must be resilient in the face of setbacks and challenges. A resilient mentality involves learning from failure, recovering swiftly, and having a positive attitude.

- **Creativity:** to stand out in a competitive industry or niche, you must be creative and original. This means thinking outside the box, experimenting with new ideas, and being prepared to take calculated risks.

- **Accountability:** you have to be in control of your activities, hold yourself responsible for your goals and objectives, and be accountable to your partners or stakeholders. This implies being open, following through

Cultivating an Entrepreneurial Mindset

on pledges, and making choices based on facts and evidence.

- **Decisiveness:** You must make swift, informed judgments to keep ahead of the competition. This means getting relevant information, considering the benefits and drawbacks, then acting decisively and confidently.

- **Persuasive communication skills:** you must be able to successfully interact with your stakeholders, which includes customers, investors, and staff. This means expressing ideas effectively and eloquently, developing connections, and understanding people's needs and motivations.

- **Intrinsic motivation and drive:** you have to be motivated by a love for your job and a feeling of purpose beyond financial gain. Intrinsic motivation is characterized by a strong desire to make a difference and provide value and a readiness to go above and beyond to accomplish your objectives.

Discovering and strengthening an entrepreneurial mindset requires ongoing effort. It takes more than luck or a dream to succeed in business and entrepreneurship. From gaining the right knowledge to maintaining the right attitude, having an entrepreneurial attitude demands hard work, but it's worth it. The possibilities for success are endless when you have that spirit of self-sufficiency, creativity, and tenacity within. You don't have to start a business to engage your entrepreneurial personality either – whether you volunteer in the community or join a professional organization, any collaborative project allows you to exercise those qualities necessary for success. Keep motivated and remember: you can make it happen if you think big and have the creativity to carry it out.

How Viable is Your Business

Business viability refers to your ability to survive and thrive in the long run. It is not only about making a profit today but also about developing a long-term model that can withstand market and economic fluctuations. A viable business, in other words, can adapt, innovate, and grow over time.

The concept of viability is even more important for online businesses. The digital world is constantly changing with fierce competition. Your online business must be agile, customer-focused, and technologically inclined to remain relevant and profitable. This means investing in the appropriate tools, platforms, and strategies to attract and keep customers, simplify processes, and remain ahead of the competition.

Why is it important to assess your business viability?

Assessing your business viability is essential because it helps you and your stakeholders to determine if the business is on the right course for long-term success. Making informed decisions regarding future investments, growth, and strategy is impossible without a thorough grasp of the business's financial and operational performance.

You may discover areas of strength and weakness and make improvements from assessing viability. For example, if a

Cultivating an Entrepreneurial Mindset

business is failing to make profits, the owner may need to rethink its pricing strategy, cut expenses, or look for new income sources. On the contrary, if the business is fast expanding, the owner may need to invest in new personnel, equipment, or marketing to maintain its pace.

Additionally, assessing viability may help businesses attract investors, get financing, and form partnerships. Investors and lenders want to see that a business has a solid strategy for success and a history of making sound decisions. You can increase your credibility and appeal to potential partners by presenting data demonstrating your business viability.

Test for determining business viability

A thorough analysis of your business viability is required to assess its long-term potential. Several factors contribute to a business's ability to survive and thrive, and it's crucial to measure these critical components to make informed future decisions.

Let us look at eight important business viability tests. These tests will be a foundation for assessing your business strengths, weaknesses, and potential opportunities. You can better understand the business's financial, operational, and strategic capability by taking a comprehensive approach to assessing viability.

This approach allows you to discover possible areas for improvement and develop a strategy for long-term success.

- **Uniqueness:** the uniqueness test determines if your business has a distinguishing selling feature or a unique value proposition that sets it apart. A one-of-a-kind product or service can help a business capture a larger market share, build a loyal customer base, and create barriers to entry for new competitors.

- **Upstart Funds:** upstart funds measure a business's access to external capital. This test determines whether the business has access to venture capitalists, angel investors, or other funding sources. The availability of start-up money might indicate the possibility of development and expansion.

- **Customer:** the customer test evaluates your business's ability to attract and retain customers. A viable business must have a clear understanding of its target market as well as a strategy for reaching out to new markets and meeting its needs. You can determine if your products and services meet customer expectations by monitoring client acquisition, retention, and satisfaction rates.

- **Competition:** the competition test looks at your business's market position and the level of competition it confronts. This test helps you identify your business strengths and weaknesses and the potential for diversity or market growth.

- **Economic mood:** the economic mood test investigates the general status of the economy and how it may affect

Cultivating an Entrepreneurial Mindset

your business operations. Interest rates, inflation, customer confidence, and other economic indicators are included. Understanding the economic environment may help you prepare for future threats and opportunities.

- **Timing:** this determines if the market is prepared to accept your products or services. Timing determines if your business enters the market at the appropriate time and whether your products or services align with current trends or customer wants.

- **Marketing:** the marketing test assesses the ability of your business to reach its target demographic successfully. This check involves a review of your business's branding, message, and marketing initiatives. Successful marketing may help your business to build a strong brand identity, increase client loyalty, and increase revenues.

- **Continuing Cash Flow:** this test evaluates the company's capacity to produce recurring revenue and manage cash flow. Revenue growth, profitability, and cash reserves are all factors to consider. A profitable business requires a sustainable cash flow plan that can support continuous operations and investments.

Ultimately, launching a business requires dedication and commitment to succeed. You should consider all the factors that make up a viable business idea – market trends, customer demand, your experience and capabilities, and the business's financials. If you've gathered enough evidence to verify a reasonable probability of success for your business idea, it's time to take the plunge. After careful research and analysis, only then will you know for sure if your business idea is truly viable.

Conducting Product and Market Research

What exactly is product research?

Product research is gaining knowledge about a proposed product to establish its feasibility and possible commercial success. Analyzing customers' preferences, researching competitors and their products, identifying trends and opportunities, and testing and refining the product concept is all part of the process. Product research can help you develop products that meet your target market's needs while standing out in a crowded online marketplace.

Why do you need product research?

It is an important part of the product development process because it helps you understand your customers' needs, preferences, and behaviors. By conducting extensive research, you can reduce the risk of developing products that do not resonate with the target mark. It will increase your possibility of developing products that meet customer needs and differentiate yourself from competitors.

Cultivating an Entrepreneurial Mindset

Product research can also help you identify new market opportunities and trends, refine product design and features, and make data-driven decisions that lead to improved product performance and profitability. Whether it's a new product or an update to an existing one, product research is an important stage to help you make informed decisions and succeed in a competitive marketplace.

Elements of product research

The various elements of product research are:

- **Market research:** this is the process of gathering and evaluating information about the market where your business operates, such as competition information, trends, and client demands. This type of research can help you make informed decisions about product development strategies, pricing, and marketing efforts.

- **Customer research** involves collecting data about consumers' habits, interests, and wants to understand their viewpoints better and uncover chances for product enhancement. This research, which may be carried out via surveys, focus groups, or other methods, can give useful insights into how consumers engage with a product and what they value the most.

- **New product development:** the process of creating and bringing a new product or service to the market is known as new product development. Product research is an important component of this process because it can help you better understand customer needs, identify market opportunities, and make data-driven decisions about product design and features.

- **Segmentation research:** in market research, a target market is segmented into smaller subgroups based on commonalities in demographics, behavior, and preferences. This research can help you better understand your customers, develop targeted marketing campaigns, and develop products that meet each segment's unique needs.

- **Concept testing:** this means getting input from prospective clients on a new product concept or idea. This type of research can help you refine your product ideas, identify potential problems or challenges, and make data-driven product development decisions.

- **Name research:** this involves collecting information about prospective product names and testing them with target consumers. This research will help you choose memorable, easy-to-say, and appealing product names for their target market.

- **Feature research:** identifying the features and functionalities consumers value most in a product and incorporating these features into product design is what feature research means. This research helps you develop products that satisfy your customers' needs while distinguishing you from the competition.

Cultivating an Entrepreneurial Mindset

- **Price research:** this means studying consumer perceptions of product value and testing multiple price points to determine the ideal pricing for a product. This research helps you price your products competitively while maintaining profitability.

Now that you understand what you need to consider while conducting product research let's look at market research.

What is market research?

This is the process of acquiring information and insights into a certain market to help you make informed decisions before launching a business. This study might involve examining the market size, growth rate, trends, opportunities, competition, price, and distribution channel information.

Market research can help you identify market gaps, understand the needs and preferences of your consumers, and develop efficient marketing strategies. You can use data-driven insights from market research to make informed decisions to help you stay competitive and flourish in the market.

Performing market research - how to get information

This is done in two ways: primary research (direct from consumers, surveys, focus groups) and secondary research (existing reports, statistics, databases) may be used to get information for market research. Primary research is tailored to particular study goals, but secondary research is often less expensive and faster to get.

Various ways of conducting market research

Market research employs various methods to collect data, including face-to-face interviews, focus groups, phone research, survey research, and internet market research. Each research method has its advantages and may give you significant insights into consumer behavior and preferences.

- **Face-to-face interviews:** people are interviewed in person to get in-depth information on their beliefs, habits, and preferences. This method is good for qualitative research and delving into difficult issues.

- **Focus groups:** small group conversations that allow participants and researchers to engage each other. It is used to gather qualitative data to uncover common beliefs, behaviors, or attitudes.

- **Phone research:** data is collected by making direct phone calls to respondents. It is quite inexpensive and can accommodate a high sample size.

- **Survey research:** data is collected using surveys, which may be sent through the mail, phone, internet, or in-person. It is convenient for gathering vast amounts of quantitative data.

- **Online market research:** data collection using online channels like surveys, social media, web analytics, and online focus groups. It is inexpensive and may swiftly gather data from a widely distributed audience.

How to Start Creating a Domain Name and Website

Developing a domain name and website can be confusing. Especially if you are starting from scratch or have limited knowledge of the web development process. Don't worry – there is hope! With effort, determination, and guidance, you can take your creative ideas into reality and create an effective website with a catchy domain name that will draw in customers. I will share my top tips on how you can develop your unique domain name and website that's perfect for your online business.

What is a domain name?

Your website's name is its domain name. The address Internet visitors can access your website is known as a domain name. It is a human-readable system of navigating a website with a name and a top-level domain extension such as .com,.org, or.net.

Domain names, which may be bought and registered via a domain name registrar, are used to find and identify websites on the internet. These are critical components of creating an online presence and developing a brand identity for both businesses and individuals.

How to get a domain name

Registering a domain name is a necessary step in building your online presence. Businesses and individuals may build a professional and trustworthy online presence that is easy to remember and access by acquiring a domain name.

Below are various procedures for registering a domain name:

- **Choose a reliable domain registrar:** GoDaddy, Namecheap, or Google Domains are all good places to start. These companies are called domain name registrars.

- **Look up your domain name:** using the registrar's search engine, find out whether your selected domain name is available.

- **Finalize your domain name selection:** if you've found an available domain name that meets your requirements, choose that.

- **Choose a domain suffix:** choose a domain name suffix (domain name extension), such as .com, .net, or .org, that best fits the purpose and aims of your website. Note that a .com is the most popular domain name extension and is considered more trustworthy.

If the domain is already taken you can simply search for a different available name. However, if you want to buy a domain name that another user has already registered, enter the registered domain name into your web browser and visit

Cultivating an Entrepreneurial Mindset

the website: Explore the domain to confirm whether it is a parked domain or already in use.

- **Get the owner's contact information if it's not a parked domain:** get the owner's contact information and make a purchase bid for the domain.

- **Negotiate a fair price for both of you:** negotiate a reasonable and acceptable price for both sides.

- **Get the domain name:** to purchase a domain name, just add it to your shopping cart, complete the required fields, and submit payment.

- **Add domain ID protection:** try adding domain ID protection to your registration. This will help keep your personal information private and safe.

- **Renew the domain name:** to retain ownership, renew the domain name before it expires.

- **Link your domain to a CMS (content management system):** to start developing your website, connect the domain name to a CMS such as WordPress, Squarespace, or Shopify.

By following these steps, you can register a domain name or buy an existing one for your business website and develop a professional, reputable, and identifiable online presence.

What to do after purchasing a domain name

Following purchasing a domain name, the next step is to obtain a hosting plan to connect your website to the internet. Without hosting your domain name, you can't build your website. This includes choosing a web hosting provider, choosing a hosting package that meets the needs of your website, and linking your domain name to your hosting account. Here's a step-by-step guide on how to host your website after purchasing a domain name:

- **Purchase a hosting plan:** choose a web hosting company and a hosting package that meets the needs of your website. Numerous hosting options are available, such as shared hosting, WordPress hosting, VPS hosting, and cloud hosting. Some hosting companies to consider are Bluehost, Namecheap, HostGator, etc. You can read online reviews about the best hosting companies and what makes them unique and make an informed decision.

- **Link the domain name to your web hosting account:** connect your domain name to your hosting account by entering the nameservers or directing the domain to the IP address of your hosting account. Most hosting companies have training videos that will take you through the process step-by-step.

- **Set up your website:** depending on your technical skills, you can use a website builder or WordPress to create your website. A website builder allows you to build your website through a drag-and-drop process. However,

Cultivating an Entrepreneurial Mindset

WordPress gives you greater control over the design and operation of your website. If you don't have the technical skills to build your website, you can hire a website developer on Fiverr or Upwork to do it for you.

- **Create new pages for your website:** create pages that provide information about your business or services, such as an about page, a contact page, Terms & Conditions, Privacy Policy, and a services page.

- **Create email accounts with your new domain:** to give your website or business a professional look, create email accounts with your new domain.

- **Submit your new website to search engines:** to help

   visitors locate your website, submit it to search engines like Google, Bing, and Yahoo.

- **Advertise your website:** to get visitors and boost your online presence, use social media, email marketing, and search engine optimization.

By following these steps, you'll be able to launch your business on the internet and ready to do business with people worldwide.

Identifying your Target Market (Analyzing the Market)

Defining your target market is an important stage in any business's success. Studying the market allows you to understand your customer's interests and behavior better, enabling you to customize your marketing strategy and increase sales.

What exactly is a target market?

A target market is a defined set of customers a business wishes to attract with its products or services. Knowing your target market is important for your business success since it helps you to personalize your marketing plans to your audience's needs and preferences. By determining your target market, you can develop successful marketing strategies to reach your ideal customers and accomplish your business goals.

Advantages of target market research

The following are some of the advantages of target market research:

- Helps in identifying customer needs and preferences.
- Increases consumer satisfaction and engagement.
- Allows for efficient market targeting and segmentation.
- Lowers marketing expenditures while increasing returns.
- Increases brand awareness and trustworthiness.
- Facilitates product creation and innovation.

Cultivating an Entrepreneurial Mindset

- Helps in identifying new market prospects.

- Improves risk management and decision-making.

- Customer retention and loyalty are increased.

- Helps in gaining a competitive advantage in the market

How to find your target market

Here are some important ways to determine your target market:

- **Evaluate your offerings:** start by studying your products or services to determine what they provide and for whom they are best suited. This will help you figure out the major advantages of your products or services and who will appreciate them the most.

- **Do market research:** learn about your target market's demands, habits, preferences, and problems. This may be accomplished via surveys, web research, and other market data sources.

- **Develop client profiles and market segments based on your research:** these should represent your ideal customers' qualities, habits, and interests. This will help you identify the most potential target audiences for your products or services.

- **Examine the competition:** analyze your competitors to learn about their strengths, weaknesses, and market positioning. This can help you identify market gaps that you may leverage to separate yourself from the competition.

By understanding the values and challenges of your target market, you can create marketing campaigns tailored specifically to their needs. This will show them that you value their opinions and beliefs, which in turn can help promote loyalty and brand advocacy. Additionally, developing a deep understanding of your target market will ensure that you develop the right products or services to maximize demand and stock up on the latest trends.

Identifying your target market is a powerful business strategy rooted in research-driven analysis that provides valuable insights from which any business can benefit greatly. Taking this necessary step is one choice that could be the difference between success and failure when competing against giant corporations within an oversaturated marketplace.

Writing a Strategic Business Plan

A business plan is a written document that covers a business's objectives, strategy, and activities. It gives a detailed summary of the products or services of the business, target market, competitors, management structure, and financial predictions. A business plan is necessary when starting and expanding a business. It helps identify the main ingredients required for success, anticipate possible problems, and develop a road map for accomplishing business goals. Below are some important things to include in a business plan.

Executive Summary

The executive summary, which is generally one-two pages long, is a quick outline of the whole business plan. It should include a synopsis of the company's idea, target market, competitive environment, and financial predictions. Since the executive summary is the first thing a prospective investor or partner reads, you must create a positive first impression.

Explain your business

This portion of your business plan should fully summarize your business history, goals, and vision. It should include information on the company's structure, ownership, and management team. It should also include patents, trademarks, or other intellectual property details.

Market analysis

The market analysis section should thoroughly examine the industry, target market, and competitors. This should involve an examination of market size, prospective growth, trends, and the competitive environment. The objective is to offer a thorough insight into the industry while also identifying opportunities and challenges.

Management and organizational structure

The section on management and organization should include a full summary of the management team, including their positions, duties, and experience. It should also provide details about the organizational structure and any advisory boards or external consultants.

List of your products and services

This section should include a full summary of the products and services of your business. It should detail each product's or service's qualities and advantages, as well as how they satisfy the target market's needs. It should also include patents, trademarks, or other intellectual property details.

Customer Segmentation

The customer segmentation section should thoroughly

summarize the target market's demographics, habits, and demands. It should identify the various segments within the target market and explain how the business intends to target and service each group.

Marketing strategy

The marketing strategy, including the marketing mix, should be specified in the marketing plan section (product, price, promotion, and place). It should include the primary strategies the company will use to reach its target market and meet its marketing goals.

Logistics and operations plan

Cultivating an Entrepreneurial Mindset

This should include a complete description of the business's activities, such as the manufacturing process, supply chain, and distribution strategy. It should also include details on the facilities, equipment, and technology required to run the business.

Financial strategy

This section should include a full analysis of the business's financial expectations, such as income, costs, and cash flow. It should thoroughly analyze the financial needs and how the business intends to utilize the cash to accomplish its goals. It should also include a clear assessment of the risks and assumptions that underpin the financial estimates.

Creating a business plan is an important step in starting and building a successful business. A well-written business plan can

help you to identify the important aspects required for success, anticipate possible challenges, and create a path for accomplishing your business goals. The nine processes listed above give a thorough foundation for creating a successful business plan.

Examine the Competition

Analyzing competition will help you identify your competition, assess your strengths and weaknesses, and utilize this knowledge to enhance your business.

What is Competitive Analysis?

It is the process of identifying and measuring the strengths and weaknesses of present and future competitors in a certain market. It involves collecting and evaluating data about competitors' products or services, marketing approaches, customer base, and other pertinent elements to acquire insights into their business operations and market positioning. The purpose of a competitive analysis is to guide you in making strategic decisions by identifying opportunities and risks in the competitive market. It will also help you to build successful marketing strategies for your business that will distinguish it from competitors and give you a competitive advantage.

Advantages of competitive analysis for online businesses

Competitive analysis may be very beneficial to online businesses. Here are some of the primary benefits:

- **Identify competition:** by doing a competitive analysis, you can learn about your competitors' products or services, marketing, and pricing strategies. This information keeps you updated on your competitive environment so that you can change your strategies appropriately.

- **Understanding market trends:** competitive analysis can also help you recognize market trends and changes. You can uncover changes in client preferences, new products or

Cultivating an Entrepreneurial Mindset

services, and new trends in marketing tactics by analyzing your competitors' activity. This data helps you stay ahead of the competition and adapt to changing market conditions.

- **Identify opportunities:** competitive analysis can also help you to identify potential growth opportunities. For example, you can develop new products or services that provide a unique value proposition by identifying market gaps or areas where competitors are not addressing customer needs.

- **Improve customer service:** you can draw from the successes and failures of your competitors and use this knowledge to improve your customer service. You can identify areas for improvement and differentiate yourself from your competitors by analyzing competitors' customer feedback and reviews.

- **Monitor industry standards:** competitive analysis can also help you in staying current with industry standards and best practices. You can be sure that you are keeping to best practices and getting a competitive advantage by monitoring your rivals' activity and following industry trends.

Overall, competitive analysis is useful for online businesses to keep informed about their competitive environment, uncover development potentials, and enhance overall strategy and customer service.

Areas competitive competition covers

The competitive analysis encompasses a range of topics, including price, search marketing, product selection, and website design. Here's a rundown of each area:

Pricing: this is an important part of competitive analysis since it directly influences a business's sales and profitability. You can analyze your competitors' pricing methods and modify their prices to stay competitive and attract consumers.

Search Marketing: this encompasses strategies such as search engine optimization (SEO) and pay-per-click (PPC) advertising, which are used to increase a business exposure in search engine results pages (SERPs). You can get insights into the keywords and ad text that generate traffic and sales for your competitors by researching their search marketing strategies and utilizing this knowledge to improve your search marketing campaigns.

- **Product selection:** another area where competitive research can give you significant insights is product selection. You find market gaps or places where you can distinguish yourself by delivering unique goods or services

  by researching your competitors' product offerings.

- **Website design:** Website design is an important part of internet business since it affects your brand image and user experience. You can get insights into best practices and design trends by researching your competitors' website

Cultivating an Entrepreneurial Mindset

designs and then utilize this knowledge to improve your website design and user experience.

By studying your competitors' strategies and performance in these areas, you can get useful insights that can shape your strategies and help you remain competitive in the market.

How to conduct a competitive analysis

To perform a successful competitive analysis, you can follow some of the steps below:

- **Determine the products or services to be evaluated:** start by defining the particular products or services for which you wish to conduct competitive research. This helps narrow your research and ensure that you compare apples to apples.

- **Identify direct competitors:** direct competitors are businesses offering the same or comparable products or services as yours. Search for these companies online, read trade journals, or conduct a poll.

- **Identify indirect competitors:** indirect competitors are companies that provide comparable goods or services to yours but are not direct competitors. A gourmet restaurant, for example, may see a fast-food chain as an indirect competitor since they both sell food.

- **Examine replacement competitors:** replacement competitors are companies that provide other solutions to the same problem or need. A bike company, for example, may see a vehicle maker as a replacement competition since they both offer a means of mobility.

- **Determine which aspects of your competitors' operations should be investigated:** not all aspects of your competitors are similar to yours. Concentrate on areas that will directly impact your business, such as price, product selection, and customer service.

- **Analyze all identified competitors:** examine your competitors' websites, social media pages, promotional materials, and customer reviews to learn more about them. You might also do surveys, focus groups, or buy their items to get direct experience.

- **Document your research in a written analysis**: prepare a comprehensive document that summarizes your research and findings and analyze the strengths and weaknesses of your competitors. This should help you make business choices and develop a strategy.

- **Identify areas to improve and implement the changes:** look at areas where your business can improve based on your findings, and then implement the changes to enhance these areas. For example, your competitors may have a better website design or quicker delivery times.

- **Keep track of your progress:** track your business performance and compare it with your competitors to assess the effect of your changes. This will allow you to assess the efficacy of your efforts and find areas for improvement.

Determining your Business Structure

The legal and organizational framework under which your business functions is referred to as the business structure. It establishes the obligations and liabilities of the business owners, how the business is managed and regulated, and how profits are shared. Choosing the correct business structure is important for every entrepreneur or business owner since it affects the business tax duties, legal responsibilities, and overall performance.

In this section, I'll thoroughly overview the various business structures, including sole proprietorship, partnership, corporation, and LLC. We'll also discuss the benefits and disadvantages of each structure, as well as the legal requirements for each and the factors to consider when deciding on the best structure for your business.

By the end of the section, you will have a good understanding of the many business structures available and can make an informed decision on which one best meets your needs.

Types of business entity

Here, you will find information about the most common types of business entities.

Sole proprietorship

A sole proprietorship is the most common type of business structure. The business is owned and controlled by a single person. The owner is personally liable for all the company's obligations and liabilities.

Advantages

- The setup is easy and affordable
- Complete control of the business
- Easy tax filing

Disadvantages

- Owner's liability is limitless
- Limited capital access
- Limited lifespan (business dies if the owner dies)

Legal requirements

- Obtain all required permits and licenses
- Register for taxes
- Follow all local, state, and federal rules

Cultivating an Entrepreneurial Mindset

Tax implications

- The proprietor discloses company revenue and costs on their tax return

- The proprietor is liable for self-employment tax

Partnership

This is business structure owned and run by two or more people; the partners share the profits and losses.

Advantages

- The setup is simple and affordable

- Responsibilities and resources are shared

- Easy tax filing

Disadvantages

- Partners' responsibility is unlimited

- Possibility of squabbles and conflicts

- Lifespan is limited (the business may cease to exist when a partner dies or leaves the business)

Legal requirements

- Draft a partnership contract

- Obtain all required permits and licenses
- Register for taxes
- Follow all local, state, and federal rules

Tax implications

- It does not pay income tax
- On their tax return, each partner discloses their share of the profits and losses
- Each partner is personally liable for self-employment taxes

Corporation

A corporation is a distinct legal entity from its owners. The shareholders elect a board of directors to run the business.

Advantages

- Owners have limited liability
- Ability to raise funds via the sale of shares
- Perpetual existence (business keeps running even if there is a change in ownership)

Disadvantages

- Expensive and difficult to set up

Cultivating an Entrepreneurial Mindset

- Double taxation (corporate income is taxed, and dividends are taxed again when distributed to shareholders)

- Strict guidelines and requirements

Legal requirements

- File articles of incorporation with the state

- Assemble a board of directors

- Follow all state and federal rules

Tax implications

- The company files and pays income taxes

- Shareholders pay taxes on dividends earned

Limited Liability Company (LLC)

A limited liability company (LLC) is a hybrid business type that combines the benefits of a corporation and a partnership. Members have limited responsibility and are the proprietors.

Advantages

- Owners have limited liability

- Pass-through taxes (company revenue is recorded on individual tax returns)

- Management and ownership flexibility

Disadvantages

- More expensive to establish than a single proprietorship or partnership

- Some states have a high level of complexity

- Lifespan is limited (business may dissolve if a member leaves or dies)

Legal requirements

- File articles of incorporation with the state

- Prepare a business contract

- Follow all state and federal rules

Tax implications

- The LLC has the option of being taxed as a partnership or a corporation

- The LLC may be subject to self-employment tax

Considerations When Choosing a Business Structure

Cultivating an Entrepreneurial Mindset

Selecting the correct business structure is crucial for every entrepreneur or company owner. The choice of an entity may influence the business's legal and financial responsibilities and its long-term viability. As a result, it is important to evaluate various aspects before settling on a company structure. In this regard, consider the following factors while deciding on a corporate structure:

Legal liability

One of the most important issues to consider when deciding on a business structure is legal liability. The extent of liability varies amongst corporate organizations, so selecting a structure with the required level of legal protection is critical. A single proprietorship, for example, gives no legal protection, but a corporation provides limited liability protection to its stockholders.

Tax implications

Another important issue to consider when deciding on a company structure is the tax ramifications. The tax obligations and implications vary depending on the kind of company entity. Some businesses, such as sole proprietorships, partnerships, and limited liability corporations (LLCs), are pass-through entities, meaning the company revenue is reported on the owners' tax returns. Corporations, on the other hand, are independent taxable entities that are liable to double taxation.

Cost of formation and ongoing administration

Another important issue when selecting a company structure is the creation and continuing administration cost. The difficulty and expense of establishing and operating various business organizations vary. A sole proprietorship, for example, is the simplest and least expensive structure, while corporations are more complicated and costly to organize and operate.

Flexibility

Another important thing to consider when choosing a company structure is flexibility. Some company arrangements, such as LLCs, provide more management, ownership, and structural freedom than corporations or partnerships. Choosing a structure that meets the firm's demands while also allowing for future development and expansion is critical.

Future requirements

When deciding on a corporate structure, it is equally critical to consider future demands. A corporate structure should be adaptable enough to handle future business developments, such as new partners, investors, or market growth. It's also critical to think about the exit plan, whether it's a sale or a transfer of ownership since various corporate forms offer different alternatives.

Finally, selecting the correct business structure is a critical choice that may affect a company's legal and financial responsibilities as well as its long-term performance. Given the aforementioned insights, business owners and entrepreneurs are better equipped to make well-informed judgments and choose the most appropriate organizational structure to achieve their goals and objectives.

Knowing the Legalities Involved

In this session, we will review the most important e-commerce laws to be aware of when running an online business. These regulations cover taxes, payment gateways, trademarks, patents, copyrights, shipping limitations, inventories, age limits, company insurance, licenses and permits, PCI compliance, and consumer privacy.

Important E-commerce Legislation You Should Know:

Taxes:

Customers in states where an online firm has a physical presence are compelled to pay sales tax.

The sales tax regulations differ per state, and it is important to remain up to current on the changes.

Payment gateways:

To accept client payments, e-commerce enterprises must employ secure payment gateways.

To guarantee safe transactions, payment gateways should

adhere to PCI DSS (Payment Card Industry Data Security Standard).

Copyright, patents, and trademarks:

Online sellers must guarantee that their goods, services, and website content do not violate trademarks, patents, or copyrights.

Before employing any intellectual property, it is essential to get legal guidance and due diligence.

Shipping restrictions:

Shipping restrictions may apply to some items, such as hazardous materials, guns, and pharmaceuticals.

Online business owners must be aware of shipping constraints for their items and follow the rules.

Inventory:

Business owners must keep correct inventory records and follow product labeling and packaging standards.

Maintaining stock level tracking is critical to minimize stockouts and overstocks.

Age restrictions:

Certain items, such as cigarettes, alcohol, and adult material, may have age limitations.

Cultivating an Entrepreneurial Mindset

Online businesses must adhere to age limitations and check the

age of their clients.

Business insurance:

To safeguard against obligations and hazards, online enterprises should consider purchasing business insurance.

It is critical to understand the insurance policies' coverage and exclusions.

Permits and licenses:

State and local governments may require licenses and permits for online businesses.

It is critical to obtain the necessary licenses and permits and to follow all regulations.

PCI DSS compliance:

To ensure secure transactions, online businesses that accept credit card payments must adhere to the PCI DSS standards.

You must operate with a payment gateway that adheres to PCI DSS regulations.

Customer privacy:

Online businesses must follow privacy rules and safeguard their consumers' personal information.

Before collecting and utilizing personal information from consumers, it is critical to have a privacy policy in place and gain their permission.

Chapter Four

Accounting and Financing

Welcome to the accounting and finances chapter. I know that dealing with the financial aspects of a business can be intimidating, especially if you're just starting. But don't worry. I'm here to guide you through this process and make it as stress-free as possible. In this chapter, I'll provide an overview of the different types of accounting and financial concepts involved in running an online business. We'll also explore some tools available to help you manage your finances better. Finally, we'll discuss some of the best software that makes accounting easy. So, let's get started!

Startups Costs

Starting an online business might be an exciting prospect. However, it's not something you delve into without counting the cost. Even though launching an online business is relatively cheaper and easier than starting a brick-and-mortar business, they require some investment. Like physical businesses, there is a startup cost, and understanding the cost implications of each aspect of your online business can help you make accurate projections that could help you successfully run your online business.

The costs include business license, web hosting, web design and responsiveness, e-commerce platform, payment processing, inventory, marketing, PPC marketing, web content creation, and social media. Let's look at each of these costs separately.

1. **Business License**

Many people don't know this, but you require a license to operate an online business much the way a brick-and-mortar store does. For instance, you might need to register for sales tax. Alternatively, you might need a particular license for a profession or occupation to complete your work. A general business license or a license for weights and measurements may also be required. Each state and district have different requirements for permits.

2. **Web hosting**

You must get a domain name and web hosting to run a successful online business. Previously, we covered getting your domain name and hosting up and running. Your web hosting charges will depend on the amount of traffic coming to your site. You can pay your hosting fees either monthly or annually.

3. **Web design and responsiveness**

We cannot overemphasize the need to have a mobile-friendly website. Many customers now use their phones to make

Accounting and Financing

purchases online. So, you must build a mobile-friendly website. Also, the website has to be built following brand colors and fonts. Hire a professional web designer who has experience building e-commerce sites. This will ensure that all features and pages will be present. Professional web designers usually charge a good fee for their service. However, it won't put a hole in your pocket.

4. **E-commerce platform**

E-commerce platforms are software applications designed to assist business owners in creating and managing online stores, processing product payments, and tracking inventory. These platforms are frequently cloud-based and typically require a monthly fee for usage. The fees can depend on the specific features and tools the business owner requires.

5. **A payment processor**

You must integrate a payment processor into your online store to ensure you get paid when people buy your products or services online. Payment processors and the amount they charge to accept credit and debit cards vary depending on the card type, the amount of sale, and which processor you decide to employ. Discover, Visa, and Mastercard charges a fee ranging from 1.5% to 2.5%, whereas American Express charges a fee of 2.5% to 3.5%. Additionally, the payment processor adds another fee called the "markup," which varies and is open to negotiation.

6. **Inventory and inventory shrinkage**

No matter the kind of business you are doing, you would need to stock inventory. Many online business owners say that inventory takes up a sizable percentage of their costs. Inventory cost is simply the amount to store, maintain, and restock the products. Inventory shrinkage is another important consideration. Goods get damaged in transit or storage sometimes. Also, there might be errors due to miscalculations. All of these factors have to be considered.

7. Drop-shipping

Many business owners choose to avoid inventory costs. Instead, they could decide only to order the products when a customer makes an order. Still, there are costs incurred with this model. The sales platform you use might charge a fee for listing your products. Sometimes, it's a flat fee. Other times, it's a percentage of your sale. This can quickly eat into your profit.

8. Marketing

Marketing is one of the most important costs you can incur. Marketing involves getting your products or services in the eyes of those that need them. Marketing costs can include search engine optimization (SEO), PPC ads, social media promotions, and content creation. Search engine optimization ensures that potential customers get to see your offering. These costs are often high as setting up a website to rank high on the search engines takes a lot of work, including building backlinks and optimizing your website's content.

Accounting and Financing

9. Web content creation

In the digital marketplace, content is king! If you are not

proficient at content creation, you would need to spend money hiring freelancers to craft you top-notch content that would rank you highly organically on search engines, engage your website visitors, and convert them into paying customers. Many search engines use algorithms that assess the quality of content and its relevance and use this to rank them. Quality content creators are not cheap. So, you might need to spend money hiring content creators to help you produce high-quality and engaging content.

10. Social media

Social media is fast becoming an avenue for online businesses to make sales. Chances are that you are not skilled in handling the aspects of content creation, monitoring reviews, and running social media ads, which your business social media handles need. You might need to employ a professional social media expert to handle this side of your business. You can hire professional social media managers from reputable freelance platforms like Upwork and Fiverr.

These are some of the most important costs you would need to consider to run an online business successfully and make significant daily profit. The knowledge of these costs can be the defining factor in whether your business thrives or suffers.

Creating a Budget

You have to learn a lot of new skills as a small business owner.

One is how to create a business budget, which can be scary, especially if you're just starting. How exactly do you know where to find the right financial data, let alone master the terms used in business finance and organize all that information correctly?

All this may be enough to deter some people from launching a business in the first place. According to a survey, the majority of small business owners don't even start with a budget. However, if you approach it the right way, creating a business budget isn't all that difficult. You can do that in simple steps that I'll show you here.

What's a budget?

A budget is a financial plan that factors every expenditure, capital, and profit over a period. When running an online business, you want to be able to track every dollar. That's what having a budget can do for you.

There are several benefits to making a business budget. It puts your finances in check. A business budget ensures that you always have money to execute your business transactions, run expenditures, and expand your business when the opportunity arises.

Accounting and Financing

A budget also helps you achieve long-term goals. With a carefully followed business budget, you can work towards your long-term goals, cutting expenses along the way and spending wisely. This creates room for you to achieve your financial goals.

A budget can help you grow your business. One of the first

things investors look at before investing in your business is your budget (with a specific interest in income and expenditure). With a budget, you can maintain financial security. When your budget is healthy, you will not be grossly affected in times of downturn or recession. You will always be open for business.

Lastly, a budget helps you take advantage of opportunities. You will always be ready when opportunities come for expansion, unlike businesses that never have a budget and spend unwisely.

Steps to creating a business budget

Although making a budget can be intimidating, you don't need a finance or accounting background to create it. Follow these steps to create a budget for your business.

1. **Examine your revenue**

One of the first things you need to look at when drafting a budget is the revenue coming into your business. We say revenue and not profit because you have to factor in every income source before you incur expenses. Calculate your revenue over a certain period. This will give you a clear view of trends and patterns in your income over a given period, say a year. With this, you can adequately plan for a fall, so you are never found wanting or always have a cushion for a drop in income.

2. Subtract fixed costs

The next step is to add all your fixed costs and subtract the total fixed cost from your revenue. Fixed costs are those you incur regularly. It could be costs incurred daily, weekly, or monthly. Fixed costs include rent, debt repayment, taxes, payroll, insurance, etc. Once you have added them up, you subtract this sum from your revenue from the first step. Once that is done, we move to the next step.

3. Determine variable expenses

Variable expenses are not constant. Your use of them is dependent on circumstances and the current state of your business. Variable expenses are also called discretionary expenses. Usually, they help in keeping the business running. Examples of variable expenses include utilities, owner's salary, office supplies, replacing old equipment, marketing supplies, etc. During a business downturn, you might choose to lower variable expenses to stay afloat. However, during profitable months, you might choose to increase variable expenses to expand or increase the long-term profitability of your business.

4. Set aside a contingency fund for unexpected costs

Accounting and Financing

No matter how we try to avoid it, unexpected expenses will always come up. And they sometimes do so when the budget is tight. It might arise just when you are planning a summer vacation. Suddenly, there's flooding, and you would need to replace inventory. Sometimes, it's the car breaking down when you are going to buy a new gadget. It's always better to prepare for such eventualities. Rather than succumb to the temptation of spending all your profits on variable expenses, it's wise to set some aside for emergency expenses. The way it works is that when you plan for unexpected expenses, they rarely show up. But, on the rare chance that they occur, you'd be better prepared to handle them.

5. Create your profit and loss statement (P & L)

This is the place where anxiety creeps in for some online business owners. Yet, it's one of the most important steps to take in budgeting. It determines the direction your business is moving in. Here, you add all your income for the month on the one side and all your expenses for the month on the other. Next, you subtract all your expenses from the income. If the result you get is positive, it means you've made a profit for the month. However, if it's negative, you don't have to beat yourself. New businesses sometimes have unprofitable months. It only means you must take some measures to improve the result for the upcoming month.

6. Outline your forward-looking business budget

Now that you've created your P & L statement, it's time to project into the future of your business. Here, you have to study your P & L document to give you a broad view of what expenses to keep incurring and those to cut down. It helps you see patterns and seasons and how they affect your business. From your P & L, you can make inferences and better plans for the future. For example, you can understand which months are most favorable for your business and pull in the biggest profits. Also, you can have seasons when your business experiences a downturn. So, you can reduce your expenses during those periods going forward.

Knowing where you are and where you're going is crucial if you want your online business to succeed. A well-thought-out budget can serve as your guide for creating a successful and lucrative business.

Managing Your Personal Finance

Your business finance is different from your personal finance. Business finance is used to manage a business's assets, liabilities, revenues, and debts. While personal finance is the term used to describe all financial decisions and activities made by a person, including budgeting, mortgage planning, insurance, savings, and retirement planning. These two accounts should be maintained separately to make managing them easier and prevent personal cash from being used for business expenses.

As a business owner, you might be tempted to treat all business profits as personal income, but even while the money

Accounting and Financing

is in your control, it shouldn't be handled that way. This carries significant risks. One of the advantages of managing your personal finance is that it makes it easier to save money to support your family while starting a business or to save funds to finance a business. Here's how to manage your personal finance.

1. **Detail your financial goals**

Write down all your long and short-term goals. Do you plan to go on a vacation with your family all expenses paid from your business? Do you want to retire early? Is it to reduce your spending? Or make a down payment for an item? Put it all down. Then, arrange them in order of priority to you.

2. **Flesh out your plan**

Write down your plan in detail, including the plan of action. Outline your spending plan, your monthly budget, and how you can get out of debt (if that's a concern). It's important to emphasize again that you need to plan according to your priority. So, you want to start working towards your long-term goals while also fulfilling the short-term ones.

Another important thing to consider is keeping emergency funds aside. As you work on your budget, you should also work towards your goals and set aside some funds for unexpected expenses. This ensures you are not suddenly overwhelmed.

3. **Stick to your budget**

One of the most important instruments for your financial success is your budget. It enables you to make a spending plan to distribute your funds in a way that will support the achievement of your goals. Your budget can be as general or specific as you choose as long as it enables you to accomplish your main objectives of spending less than you make, eliminating any debt, increasing your emergency fund, and saving money for the future. Using a budget, you can make better financial decisions in the months and years ahead. Without a budget, you might spend money on items that may seem vital right now but don't accomplish anything to improve your future.

4. Pay off your debts

For many people, debt presents a significant barrier to achieving their financial goals. You should, therefore, make getting rid of it your priority. Create a debt repayment plan to expedite the process. Once you have paid off all your debt, commit to keeping it that way by putting measures in place to forestall falling back into debt. Keeping your credit cards at home can be a smart move. You should save money for emergencies so that you won't be tempted to use your credit card to pay for unexpected expenses.

5. Don't be afraid to ask for help

If your savings have increased and you want to start investing to expand your wealth, talk to a financial planner for advice on how to make smart investing decisions. In addition to helping

Accounting and Financing

you identify investments that fit your comfort level and investing return expectations, a professional adviser will explain the risks associated with each investment and help you to reach your goals as quickly as possible. Another benefit is that a financial planner may help you create a budget.

You have to separate business money from personal money. This separation prevents misunderstanding when dealing with taxes or other legal payments, makes you accountable for the business money, and helps you monitor your spending. This separation also protects your personal funds from business debts or liabilities if the business fails.

How Feasible is Bootstrapping?

Bootstrapping is essentially when an entrepreneur starts a business with limited resources – usually their own money or money from family and friends. This replaces the need for outside financial investments, such as venture capital or angel investors. Bootstrappers aim to grow their businesses quickly and efficiently without taking on any debt.

The key principle of bootstrapping is to focus on generating revenue from day one. This means keeping costs as low as possible and ensuring that the product or service you're offering can generate enough income to cover costs and make a profit. You should also try to find ways to automate processes, outsource tasks, or otherwise reduce overhead costs to maximize your profits.

When it comes to getting started with bootstrapping, a few key steps should be taken. First, it's important to clearly define the purpose of the business and what problem it is solving for customers. This will give you a clearer vision and help you focus on the areas where you need to spend money. You should also create a budget so you can plan out how much money you need and where it needs to be allocated.

Once the basics are in place, looking for ways to generate income quickly is important. This could mean offering special deals or discounts, creating an affiliate marketing program, or exploring other revenue-generating methods.

When it comes to how feasible bootstrapping is, the answer will

depend on a variety of factors. If you can keep costs low and generate enough income to support your business, then it can be done. However, if you don't have much experience or don't have access to funding, then bootstrapping may not be the best option for you.

Ultimately, bootstrapping is a great way to launch and grow a business without taking on debt or relying on outside funding. But it's important to do your research and ensure you understand how it works before jumping in. With careful planning and execution, bootstrapping can be a great way to get your startup off the ground and grow it into a successful business.

Accounting and Financing

So, is bootstrapping feasible? The answer is yes – with careful planning and execution, you can make bootstrapping work for your business. However, do your research and ensure you understand the basics of how it works before getting started.

Other Forms of Funding Your Business

Previously, I explained bootstrapping and how it can be an option for you, especially when you are just starting a business and want to maintain 100% control. However, there are several other options you might want to explore. That's our focus here.

Now, there are several questions that you have to answer to identify the exact funding source that fits you, including how quickly you need the funding. How much do you need? Are you looking to pay back the interest or via equity? What is the financial history of your business? Is it something that would look good to potential investors or lenders? What part of your business are you looking to finance? Once you have answered these questions, you can now identify the funding source from those listed below that fits your needs.

1. **Crowdfunding**

Crowdfunding has proven to be the method of choice for many tech startups. Through Crowdfunding, you enjoy significantly more freedom than other sources of funding.

Examples of some popular Crowdfunding platforms are GoFundMe, Kickstarter, and Indiegogo.

2. An accelerator, incubator, or mentoring program

You can be on the receiving end of some benefits when you join an incubator or accelerator program. You can find tech-based incubators almost everywhere. Also, there are online incubators available. When you join an accelerator or incubator program, you get access to resources, tools, expertise, and connections that can put you in a strong position to gain funds for your business.

3. A business line of credit

This particular funding source is best for incremental business expenses. You will discover that when you are at the beginning stage of your online business, you cannot exactly state how much funds you require for a given time. That's because there are sometimes unforeseen expenses. The business line of credit

can help you here. It is a hybrid between a bank loan and having a credit card. It allows you to withdraw funds in line with a predetermined amount of financing. You pay interest only for the amount you borrowed.

There are two types of business lines of credit. A secured line of credit and an unsecured line of credit. The secured line of credit would require that you have collateral. This kind of credit puts a little risk on the lender and so comes with a lower interest rate. However, the unsecured line of credit does not

Accounting and Financing

require collateral, but the requirements are very strict. For one, you must have a good financial record and credit rating. Also, you must prove that you are capable of generating good revenue. Another downside is that you pay higher interest rates than what's obtainable with a secured loan credit option. This type of credit funding is best for small businesses with a limited cash flow.

4. Inventory financing (purchase order financing)

Inventory financing is credit businesses obtain to pay for products not intended for immediate sale. You can use inventory finance to take out a loan against all or a portion of your inventory. The sales worth of your products will be estimated by lenders, who will then provide a loan amount based on that value and set up a repayment schedule. If you pay back the loan on time and in full, you will get your inventory back for sale.

5. SBA loan

Small Business Administration (SBA) loans offer funding for

businesses of all sizes, including online businesses. They offer a range of financing options, from short-term loans to long-term financing. This can provide your business with the funds needed to launch or expand operations. SBA loans also offer good interest rates and flexible repayment terms, which can make them an attractive option for online businesses. The downside to this type of loan is the lengthy paperwork involved and the collateral.

6. **Venture capital**

This can prove to be a good funding source for your online businesses. It makes the capital available needed to launch new products and services, improve existing ones, and fund advertising campaigns. Venture capitalists typically invest in companies with foreseeable growth potential and can provide funding in multiple stages, from seed funding to later-stage investments. This allows you to access greater sums of capital as you advance. One downside to this source of funding is decreased financial freedom.

If financing is the only thing standing in your way of starting a business, many options are available for any type of business to succeed.

Are there Shortcuts to Funding Your Online Business?

Taking shortcuts in business may appear to be a cost-effective

way to save time and money, but in the long run, it may not be worth it. Cutting corners can help you complete tasks quickly, but if the quality of the work is poor, you will likely end up having to redo it and spend more money.

For example, if you choose a free online template for your website, it may not look professional or function just the way

Accounting and Financing

you want it. You will need to spend more money on customization or hiring a professional designer.

In the same vein, when hiring an employee or freelancer, you have to consider the required skills and experience instead of going for a cheaper option. You may end up paying more to have the job done properly.

Therefore, investing time and energy into finding the right solution for your business is the best way to ensure quality results and long-term cost savings.

Your Revenue Structure

The goal of every business is to make money or maximize profit, as the experts would say. Most businesses genuinely care about their customers, and an increasing number of them are even giving back to their communities through philanthropic endeavors. But without a sustainable revenue model, a business cannot succeed.

A revenue model is simply how a business plans to make money.

It outlines how a business will yield profit by supplying goods or services, fixing prices, and managing costs. Revenue models are used to predict the potential financial success of a product or service.

There are different revenue models that an online business can adopt. Let's look at each of them.

1. **Advertising revenue model**

It's one of the most popular ways online businesses make money. It entails allowing third-party advertisers to place ads on your website or app. Each time a user clicks on an ad, you get paid. It's a terrific way to monetize your content without relying on subscriptions or other payment models. The best part of the advertising revenue model is that it's relatively simple to set up. All you have to do is build a website or app, create content, and find an ad network that works with your platform, then place their ad code on your website or app. Then, as users view and interact with the ads, you start to generate revenue. For this model, you get paid based on the number of users that see or interact with the ads. So, it's important to focus on getting more traffic to your website or app.

2. **Subscription revenue model**

This model is one of the best for generating regular monthly income for your business. In this model, you charge a reoccurring fee for accessing your services or using your products. This model has several advantages. For one, you get paid no matter how little the customer used your service within the time frame. Also, you can have a rough estimate of how much you can expect monthly. You get to establish a long-term relationship with your customers and even enjoy the benefit of returning customers occasionally.

Accounting and Financing

3. Transaction revenue model

This model involves charging a fee every time a transaction is made through your platform. An example of a business that does this is eBay. They charge sellers a fee whenever an item is sold. Also, PayPal charges their users a fee for using their platform for transactions. This model works best for businesses that process many transactions daily. So, even though the fee could be small, the profit is high because of the volume of transactions coming in daily.

4. Sales revenue model

This is a great way to make money without relying on third-party platforms. Businesses using this model come to marketplaces as common entry points for dealing with various products. Online retailers can sell their products on marketplaces for prices that compare favorably to those in a physical store or on other websites. You'll have more control over pricing, product selection, and customer data, which can help you create products and services tailored to their needs.

5. Affiliate revenue model

This is another viable business model that you can adopt. You partner with other businesses and promote their products or services on your website or blog. You get a referral sales

commission when someone clicks on the link and purchases. It's a great way to make money without producing anything yourself. Plus, you don't have to worry about customer service or fulfillment. All you have to do is ensure high-quality content that drives traffic to your affiliate links.

6. **Agency revenue model**

Agency revenue models are a convenient solution for businesses that don't have the time or resources to find the services they need. The agency acts as a middleman, connecting the client with a service provider and earning a commission. This model can provide added value by offering additional services, such as marketing and customer support, to ensure the client gets the most out of the deal. It's efficient and cost-effective, allowing businesses to access the services and products they need without managing the entire process themselves.

7. **Sponsorship revenue model**

Sponsorship revenue is an excellent online business revenue model to consider. It's a great way to generate regular income by collaborating with businesses to advertise their products and services. You can offer them a range of benefits, such as promotional posts on your website or social media accounts, blog posts, or access to exclusive content. This will help them expand their customer base and provide you with a share of their profits. It's a win-win situation. The key is to find a suitable sponsor who can be beneficial to your business and vice versa.

These are the most common kinds of revenue models you can

Accounting and Financing

adopt for your online business. You can choose one or adopt a combination of revenue models to propel your business and get you closer to achieving your business goals.

Taxes on Online Business

Taxes are an important part of every business, including those done online. You must know the different taxes that apply to your online business and how to report them. Let us examine the various taxes you need to consider when managing an online business, how to identify which taxes you need to pay, and how to keep detailed records to remain compliant with the law.

1. **Income tax**

All types of businesses are expected to pay income taxes, no matter how small. Online businesses are not exempted from this type of tax. Income tax is levied on profits. When running an online business, you'll have to determine how much you'll owe in income tax. This is typically computed by calculating your profits and making deductions, such as your business expenses. The resulting figure is then multiplied by the appropriate tax rate for your jurisdiction. You may be required to register with the IRS, pay estimated taxes, and file annual returns. You should also be familiar with the rules and regulations of the state or countries where you operate your business. Different states and countries may have different tax rates, filing requirements, and deductions. Make sure to keep accurate records of all your income and expenses. This ensures you're compliant and paying the correct amount in taxes. It will also make filing taxes easier and faster.

2. **Sales tax**

Different states have different laws concerning online sales tax. Be sure to contact your state revenue department and inquire about their tax laws for online businesses. With the right knowledge about your state's sales tax law, you can ensure compliance in collecting the right amount from each customer. It is important to note that sales tax law is based on where the customer lives rather than where the business is located.

3. **Physical location**

If your business has a physical location in a state where sales tax is required, you are typically required to collect sales tax for online sales. However, this law varies from state to state. That is why you need to know the tax laws and stay updated on the legislation because they can change at any time without information sent out to business owners.

4. **Affiliate**

If your business is built around collecting commissions from affiliate sales, then you might want to check the law on sales tax applicable in your state. Some states have enacted laws that obligate online marketers to charge and remit sales tax on products purchased from affiliates based in states where the

Accounting and Financing

law is in effect. This is irrespective of where the affiliate company exists or where the products sell. Other states may follow suit with similar legislation. So, endeavor to keep abreast of sales tax laws for online concerns in your state.

5. Sales in your state

Legislation in some states requires online businesses to collect and pay sales tax only when selling to customers in their home state, just like mail-order companies have been doing for several years. This is just an expansion of the same retail sales tax laws for internet marketers.

6. Report sales for use tax

Residents of certain states may have to pay a use tax on products purchased from out-of-state sellers if sales tax is not collected. Colorado is an example of a state that is trying to ensure compliance with this rule by passing laws requiring vendors who do business with customers in the state to file a report if the customer spends more than $500 a year.

Managing Your Tax Bracket

Understanding tax brackets is essential for managing your taxes and ensuring you are paying the right amount. Tax brackets are the levels at which the government taxes a certain percentage of your income. The higher your income, the higher bracket you'll be in, meaning you will pay a higher rate on each dollar earned.

Knowing your tax bracket can help you make smarter decisions about managing your income and planning for the future. For

example, if you're in a high-tax bracket, then it may be worth considering investing more of your money so that you can take advantage of pre-tax deductions or other strategies to lower your taxable income. On the other hand, if you're in a lower tax bracket, it may be worth investing less so that you can come out ahead on taxes.

However, there are some things you can do to minimize your taxes.

7. Use your home as the primary place of business

According to the Internal Revenue Service (IRS), if you use your home as your main business address, you may be eligible to deduct certain business-related expenses from your taxes. These include rent, internet access, office furnishings, telephone costs, and energy bills. To be eligible for these deductions, the home office must be used solely and regularly for business operations, and it must be the primary business location. Also, you must keep detailed records of all business expenditures to ensure the deductions are accurate. However, it is important to note that the IRS doesn't allow you to use these deductions to file a net loss for your business.

Accounting and Financing

8. Employ a family member

Hiring family members can be cost-effective for online business owners looking to stay within a tax bracket. By doing so, you can save money by avoiding paying the FUTA tax (Federal Unemployment Tax Act) and also provide your family members with employment and financial stability. However, you need to be aware of the rules and regulations of employing family members. You should also do research on them before making any decisions.

9. Start a retirement plan

By creating a retirement plan for yourself, you can allocate your funds tax-efficiently and reduce your yearly taxable income, ultimately keeping you in a lower tax bracket and saving you more each year. A 401k retirement plan can be a highly beneficial choice for entrepreneurs doing business online. With a 401k, you can contribute to your retirement account before taxes are deducted from your salary, significantly reducing your taxable income.

10. Save money for healthcare needs

To manage your tax bracket effectively, it is a good idea to save money for healthcare needs. One way to do this is by using Health Savings Accounts (HSAs), which offer tax benefits for medical expenses. Contributions made to an HSA are tax-deductible, and withdrawals for qualified medical expenses are tax-free. Contributing to an HSA can decrease your taxable income and potentially move into a lower tax bracket. Saving for healthcare needs through an HSA helps manage your tax bracket and provides a financial safety net to cover medical expenses when necessary.

11. Change your business structure

Changing your business structure is a possible option to manage

your tax bracket as an online business owner. You may consider transitioning to an S corporation or LLC if you are currently a sole proprietor or partnership. These business structures have pass-through taxation, which refers to businesses that do not pay taxes on the entity level. This may result in a lower tax rate and help you stay within a lower tax bracket.

12. Deduct your travel expense

Another effective way to manage your tax bracket as an online business owner is by utilizing business travel deductions. Business travel expenses can be fully deducted from your tax return, but personal travel expenses do not qualify for this benefit. However, small business owners can make the most of their business travel by combining personal travel with a justifiable business purpose.

By taking advantage of these strategies, you can reduce your taxable income and potentially move to a lower tax bracket.

Managing Your Inventory

Managing inventory is key to the success of any business. Without proper management, you can lose track of what products you have in stock when more is needed, and how much money is spent on inventory. Inventory management can help you stay organized and improve your bottom line. By closely monitoring your stock levels, you can optimize the inventory needed for operations, reduce costs from unnecessary wastage or over-investment, and better plan for future inventory needs.

Additionally, effective inventory management can help you manage customer satisfaction levels by ensuring that your stock is always available when customers order it. You can streamline operations and increase profitability by understanding the importance of managing your inventory and incorporating the right strategies into your business model. Here are some strategies to manage your inventory.

1. **Organization is crucial**

Organizing your inventory means categorizing items, establishing a tracking system, and ensuring everything is in its appropriate location. The benefits of organizing inventories are that it prevents overstocking and stockouts, enhances order fulfillment, identifies top-selling products, and makes informed restocking decisions.

2. **Upgrade to an inventory management software**

Would you believe that some big businesses manage their inventory manually with basic methods like spreadsheets or even paper and pencil? While this might be feasible for small businesses, it becomes more difficult as your business grows. Shortly, you realize that using software like excel isn't the best management option in the long term. Here's why. First, as your business grows, you find that more than one person would need to handle the inventory. With basic spreadsheet software or pen and paper, there are chances of errors occurring like illegible writing or misplaced figures. And with several people handling the inventory, a mistake is just a step away. With more sophisticated inventory software, you can handle these problems. The software can help streamline your inventory management by automating tasks such as stock tracking, purchase orders, and order fulfillment.

3. **Automate your warehouse operations with barcode scanning**

Using barcode scanning to automate warehouse operations involves assigning a unique barcode to each product in the inventory and tracking their movements using a scanner. This improves inventory accuracy, increases efficiency, and reduces errors. Barcode scanning allows for discrete and efficient fulfillment, as workers can quickly locate and pick items for shipment without manual searching.

4. **Analyze your data to drive reordering decisions**

To make informed decisions about when to reorder products for your online business, you need to use data analysis tools to examine inventory levels and sales data. Analyzing the data can help you identify which products are selling quickly, which are not moving as fast, and which are at risk of running out of stock. With this information, you can optimize inventory levels, reduce the risk of stockouts, and avoid overstocking.

5. Be vigilant and practice regular auditing

Being vigilant and conducting regular audits is crucial in managing online business inventory. Auditing involves checking

and verifying inventory records to ensure they match the available inventory. This prevents inventory errors, detects theft, and reduces the risk of stockouts or overstocking.

Your job will be much easier if you have a great inventory management system. By keeping track of your inventory with the help of the appropriate software and these methods, you may increase your profit. That ultimately translates to a satisfied client who will continue to patronize you.

Software that Makes Accounting Easy

With modern software, accounting has become more efficient and user-friendly. You can do everything from creating and managing budgets to tracking income and expenses, all within a few clicks of your mouse. It even makes filing taxes easier by providing tools like auto-filling of forms, submitting documents electronically, and more. With the right software in place, you'll be equipped to manage your finances with ease. So, here are some of the best software to consider for your financial accounting.

1. QuickBooks

Many businesses are familiar with this accounting software because of its ease of use. QuickBooks offers a range of features for its users. These features include ease of tracking income and expenses, maximizing tax deductions, invoicing, accepting payment, capturing and organization, tracking miles, tracking sales and sales tax, etc. The cloud-based software allows user access through a mobile browser or app.

Advantages

- Easy-to-use interface and navigation

- Provides an extensive range of features, such as inventory tracking, invoicing, payroll management, and expense tracking

- Integrates with multiple third-party applications to improve functionality

- Offers different pricing plans to suit businesses of all sizes

- Has exceptional customer support via live chat, phone, and email

Accounting and Financing

Disadvantages

- Limited customization options

- Some features require separate subscriptions, which may increase expenses

- Can become slow and unresponsive, especially with large data sets

- May not be ideal for businesses with complex accounting needs

- Syncing is sometimes difficult to perform

2. Xero

Xero is another good accounting software with a clean interface and allows for integration with third-party payroll services. This software was founded in 2006 in New Zealand and is fast gaining acceptance in the United States. They offer three monthly plans. One of the main advantages of Xero is its ease of use and accessibility. It can be accessed from any device with an internet connection.

Advantages

- The cloud-based software can be accessed from any location

- Simple interface that is easy to use

- Integration with various applications and software

- Has a mobile app

- Real-time monitoring of financial performance and cash flow

- Multi-currency support is available for global businesses

Disadvantages

- Some advanced features like payroll and multi-currency support are only available in higher-priced plans

- Limited customer service

- Reports have limited customization options

3. FreshBooks

With FreshBooks, users have access to a higher degree of customization when it comes to invoicing, setting it apart from other accounting software. While its primary function is to facilitate the sending, receiving, printing, and payment of invoices, it is also equipped to handle basic bookkeeping requirements. FreshBooks simplifies the invoicing process for service-based businesses by enabling them to send proposals, track project time, and receive payments.

Advantages

Accounting and Financing

- Operates on the cloud, making it easily accessible from anywhere

- Features a user-friendly interface, ensuring ease of use

- Integration with third-party apps expands its functionality

- Offers affordable pricing plans

- Provides advanced invoicing capabilities

Disadvantages

- The mobile app has limitations

4. NetSuite

This software is all about automation, which is good news for most online businesses as it can save a lot of time and relieve stress. NetSuite's automated features include things such as statement reconciliation and creating journal entries. You get insights into your business from a single dashboard, such as profitability ratios, cash positions, liabilities, fixed assets, and taxes. NetSuite's features can be accessed by custom pricing. So, a potential user is required to speak with a sales team member for a quote.

Advantages

- Provides numerous compliance features

- Automatic reconciliation and journal entries streamline accounting processes

- Accessible from anywhere, making it convenient to use

- Integrates seamlessly with other NetSuite products, such as HR, e-commerce, inventory, and order management

Disadvantages

- Pricing is not transparent

- Involves a learning curve to become proficient in using the software

5. Zoho Books

This software is one of the most comprehensive software on the market. It meets all the basic requirements of accounting software, including reconciling accounts, sending invoices, tracking expenses, and generating reports. It integrates with your e-commerce platform, payment processor, bank account, and other channels.

Advantages

- Simple and easy to use

- Automates repetitive accounting tasks such as invoicing and tracking expenses

- Syncs with bank accounts and credit cards to sync transactions

- Automatically generates financial reports

- Offers helpful customer service

Disadvantages

- Limited personalization options

- No paper-based option

- The user interface is not as sophisticated as some other accounting software

- Does not have some features found in more advanced accounting software

You can use accounting software for various tasks, such as handling tax season and managing your expenses. Every business is unique. So, choose the one that suits your specific needs.

Should You Hire a Professional

As a business owner, you need to weigh the pros and cons of hiring a professional accountant or doing your bookkeeping. On one hand, having an experienced professional handle your finances can bring greater accuracy and peace of mind that everything is being taken care of properly. On the other hand, doing it yourself allows you to stay in control and save money.

Before deciding, you need to consider the time and effort required for bookkeeping. If your business has complex financial needs or requires a lot of accounting records, hiring a professional accountant can provide invaluable assistance. Professional accountants have years of experience handling financial matters and can provide guidance and advice. They can also help save time by handling tedious tasks like data entry and reconciliations.

In addition, a professional accountant can help you with tax planning and filing so that you do not miss any important deadlines or end up paying more than necessary. Professional accountants are knowledgeable about the latest regulations and can ensure that you comply with tax laws. They can also provide valuable insight into cash flow, budgeting, and financial forecasting.

On the other hand, if your business is relatively simple or does not require frequent accounting work, then it may make sense to do your bookkeeping. The most important advantage of this approach is that you will have complete control over your finances. You will also be able to save money by avoiding the fees associated with employing a professional accountant.

Overall, deciding whether to hire a professional accountant depends on the needs of your particular business and the time

Accounting and Financing

and effort you are willing to commit to bookkeeping. It is important to weigh the pros and cons carefully before deciding. Ultimately, having an experienced professional handle your finances can provide peace of mind and save time, but it also comes with a financial cost. Whether you hire a professional or do it yourself, ensure accurate records are kept so that you can stay on top of your business.

Guide to Hiring Freelancers (Especially Virtual Assistants)

A virtual assistant (VA) is an online assistant that provides various services to businesses remotely. These services can include website design, customer service, social media management, data entry, and more. This type of assistance is a cost-effective and time-saving solution for businesses. Hiring a virtual assistant for your business might be one of the best decisions you ever make for the growth of your business.

How to Know When to Hire a Virtual Assistant

1. When you spend too much time on repetitive activities for over three months. After performing an activity regularly for more than three months, it becomes muscle memory and should be passed to a virtual assistant.

2. When you have no expertise in an area. For example, if you are not proficient in social media management and ads, you might want to employ a virtual assistant who thrives in that area.

3. When you are overwhelmed. This usually happens to new business owners. They typically spend hours from dusk to dawn and very little time on expansion. You might want to hire a VA to take care of those tasks that can go on without your presence so you can focus on other important business aspects.

Where Can You Find Virtual Assistants?

Virtual assistants have roamed the online space for a long time now. However, they can now be found in certain specific online marketplaces where they take on gigs or projects, offering their services to business owners looking for remote workers. You can find a freelancer (virtual assistant) willing to take on your project from these marketplaces. When you post your request for a virtual assistant on one of these platforms, you will receive applications from interested freelancers. You sort through these applications to choose a VA that suits your preference. Some popular marketplaces include LinkedIn Jobs, Upwork, Fiverr,

Guru, Freelancer, etc.

Steps to Hiring a Virtual Assistant

Let's look at the steps you need to take to hire a virtual assistant who's best suited for your project or task.

1. **Identify the tasks you need help with**

The first thing you need to do is to identify the areas of your business where you need an extra hand. You might need to

Accounting and Financing

take a pen and paper and outline the tasks you want your virtual assistant to handle.

2. Draft a descriptive job posting

The next step is to have a clearly defined description of the type of VA you will hire. The job posting should include details, such as ideal price range, location preference, schedule requirements, roles/responsibilities, skills required, expected experience, etc.

You want to ensure that you have this spelled out. Otherwise, you could have a barrage of applications from mostly unqualified people. Having these criteria helps greatly narrow the search, making it easier to make your pick.

3. Interview the applicants

Next, you want to set up an interview with the applicants that meet your criteria. Set up two interviews. The first would be a general interview to ensure they have fulfilled your requirements. For example, can they work from 8 am to 1 pm

EST? Kick out those that didn't meet the requirements.

In the second interview, you want to ask them specific questions about the role you will assign them. Ask for their prior work experience. Treat them as though you want to add them to your team at the office. Leave no stone unturned in picking the right candidate. It's your business we're talking about.

4. **Test the top applicants**

By now, you should have a few qualified applicants. Go ahead and set up a virtual test for them. You can use an online meeting platform like Zoom to share your screen with them and watch them perform the task you assign to them. You want to be sure they can follow instructions and are proficient with using any technology required for your business operation. Again, kick out those that cannot work in such an environment.

5. **Make your final decision**

By now, you should have just two or three applicants left. Put everything you have learned about the remaining applicants together and decide whom to hire.

You know about their previous work experience and if they can work within your time frame. Place a premium on those who did well during the screen share test. They are the ones who show they can work to your satisfaction. If you're not hiring for a one-time project, you want to hire someone who can work with you for at least six months. Ensure to state this from the beginning. You don't want to go through the hassle of finding

another virtual assistant any time soon.

Key takeaways

Accounting and Financing

- Startup costs can be a major barrier to entry for new businesses, so it's important to carefully consider all sources for funding your business.

- A budget is essential for managing your finances and ensuring that your business remains viable in the long term.

- There are several software options available that can make accounting and bookkeeping much easier for your business.

- Hiring a professional accountant or bookkeeper can be a wise investment, especially if you're not confident in your abilities.

- Taxes can be a complex issue for online businesses, so it is important to seek professional advice to ensure compliance with all applicable laws.

- Inventory management is another critical aspect of running a successful business, and some software solutions are available to help streamline this process.

- Freelancers can be a great option for businesses looking to outsource some of their work, but it's important to vet them carefully before hiring.

In the next chapter, I'll show you a roadmap for launching your online business, including building, setting up the store, and driving traffic to the online store. I call this putting yourself out there.

Chapter Five

How to Put Yourself Out There

Starting an online business can be a daunting prospect. You might feel overwhelmed when trying to understand the complexities of getting your venture off the ground and into the digital market, but don't worry – we've all been there. This blog post is designed to provide helpful tips from entrepreneurs who have 'been there and done that,' so you can successfully launch your own unique business! Read on for our roadmap for putting yourself out there and getting your enterprise up and running in no time.

Launching your New Online Business

Launching an online business has a lot of advantages. You can choose your own schedule, work from home, and concentrate on a market that interests you while often avoiding high initial fees. Even though the idea of launching a business online could be more convenient, the steps for growth and maintenance are the same as for opening a conventional or brick-and-mortar business. We shall be discussing ways you can strategically and successfully launch your new online business venture.

1. Determine and evaluate the viability of the new business idea

Evaluating and determining the possibility that the business idea becomes profitable is the first step when launching probably seems obvious. But you would be shocked at how often aspiring business owners go straight to branding or website creation before having a solid business idea in mind.

2. Start developing your business plan

Once you determine whether people might be interested in your business, you can start working on your business plan. As you've been defining and validating your idea, you've actually been putting together the first parts of your business plan. But now, you need to put it in a format you can use to get funding, make financial projections, and return to as your business grows.

3. Choose a business name

Choosing a name for your business is essential to the launching process. Your chosen name must be available for registration as a business name in your state and in the digital space, as your business will primarily operate online.

This means you must determine whether the preferred name is available as a:

How to Put Yourself Out There

- Business name in your state

- Domain name

- Username on every social media platform you intend to use

If your desired name is unavailable as a domain name or social media username, consider different variations. Remember that there are many domain name extensions beyond ".com." Furthermore, you have to check that your name and domain name are not infringing on any registered trademarks.

4. **Choose your business structure**

The legal and tax requirements you have to meet will depend on the type of business structure you choose. Most small business owners choose a structure from the list below:

- **Sole proprietorship** - This is the easiest way to set up a business. The fact that it doesn't have limited liability makes up for its simplicity.

- **Partnership** - You might like this type of business structure if you start a business with a partner. In this business structure, your liability is the same as if you were a sole proprietor.

- **Limited Liability Company (LLC)** - An LLC is one of the most common ways a small business is set up because it gives limited liability without adding the complexity of incorporation.

- **Corporation** - A corporation gives you limited liability, just like an LLC, but it's harder to set up and maintain than the other business structures. Depending on your situation, it may be a good choice.

It's always a good idea to talk to a lawyer about what kind of structure is best for your new business. Since each structure has its own tax rules, you might also want to talk to a tax expert.

5. **Handle all the necessary legal matters**

If you want your online business to have the same legal standing as a storefront, you must file the necessary business formation documents and other paperwork. Some examples are:

- Filing the necessary paperwork with local, state, and federal agencies

- Procuring any necessary permits and licenses

- Getting the necessary tax identification numbers and taking care of your tax obligations to the federal and state governments

Even though these rules vary from state to state and depend on how your organization works, you must look into them

How to Put Yourself Out There

thoroughly to ensure adequate compliance. To ensure that you're on the right track, it's always a good idea to talk to a lawyer in your industry with experience in business start-ups.

6. Create your site

Now that you have your business plan, the name, and the structure of your business and have taken care of all the legal issues, you can focus on getting your website up and running. While building your website, set up a preview landing page or "coming soon page" to announce your new product or service and pique interest. To show off your business well, you must make decisions about hosting, platform, and design. When it comes to operating an online business, your website is the best way to show what your business is all about. It needs to show your products, services, and mission accurately.

7. Create and execute your pre-launch marketing plans

Marketing your online business as you work on the other steps is essential. Your business plan should have given you the information you need to create efficient marketing strategies for your target market. Whichever strategies you use, ensure you do not skimp on implementation. You can set yourself up for a successful launch by making your target market more excited about your launch through social media and other marketing techniques.

8. Launch your new business

When you launch your website and announce your opening, you'll be "cutting the ribbon" metaphorically. You can announce your business launch in different ways, including but not limited to:

- Social media platforms
- Online press release
- Email list
- Advertisements
- Online Ads
- Etc.

Prelaunch marketing pays off during launch. These steps will give your online business a good start, but you will still have to work hard. This way, you can focus on running and marketing your new business rather than putting out fires.

E-commerce or Creating Your Domain Name

When you are ready to launch an online business, you need to choose between creating a website using an e-commerce platform or buying and registering your own domain name. There are benefits and drawbacks associated with both options, so it's important to consider the various factors when deciding which is best for you.

How to Put Yourself Out There

An e-commerce platform is an online service that provides the tools and technology to help you create and manage a website. These platforms often offer many features, such as payment processing, product management, shipping options, analytics, customer accounts, etc. Some platforms even provide built-in marketing tools to help you get started right away. The main advantage of using an e-commerce platform is that it is quick and easy to set up, so you can get your store running in no time. The biggest downside of using a platform is that you may not have full control over the design and functionality of your website.

Buying and registering a domain name for your online business gives you complete freedom to customize the design and content of your website. You also have the option to host the site on your own server, giving you full control over how it looks and operates. The downside is that setting up a domain name and hosting can be complex and time-consuming, which may not work well if you're in a hurry to launch your business.

When creating an online business, there's no one-size-fits-all solution. You need to look at each option's benefits and drawbacks and decide which is best for your needs. By carefully evaluating your goals, budget, time frame, and website requirements, you can choose the right option to help you get your store up and running quickly and effectively.

After a few years of running a successful business on e-commerce platforms, most entrepreneurs build their own websites. Some of the reasons for this are:

- They have been selling effectively on marketplaces such as Amazon, eBay, and Etsy and want to expand their business beyond that marketplace.

- They had a successful storefront or business-to-business (B2B) business for years if not decades. The low cost and ease of setting up an online storefront have convinced them to take the plunge.

- They have secured venture capital or crowd-funded money for their start-up idea, new product line, etc.

Reasons why you need an e-commerce website

There are a lot of different scenarios in which anyone would require an e-commerce website, whether you're building it on an e-commerce platform or your own website. Here are a few examples:

- **Reach out to clients worldwide:** If you run an online store, you may reach customers in any part of the world through your website. This enables you to grow your business beyond the confines of your local market.

- **Convenient shopping:** People can shop from the comfort of their homes, which is especially important in times of social isolation or if your target audience is not local.

- **Easy access to retail stores:** Customers can access your e-commerce website any time of the day or night from anywhere in the world. So, you can make money even when you're not physically present or sleeping.

- **Lower running cost:** Most of the time, the costs of running an e-commerce website are lower than those of running a traditional store. This is because you do not need to pay for rent, utilities, or employ as many people.

- **Improved insights into your customer behavior:** An

  e-commerce website may supply you with useful data about the behavior and preferences of your customers, which can help you make more informed business decisions.

- **Flexibility:** Because an e-commerce website can be updated quickly and easily, it allows you to adjust your product selection or the layout of your website as needed.

- **Advantage in the marketplace:** As more and more companies move their operations online, having an e-commerce website can give you an advantage in the marketplace over those that do not have one.

Remember that making a successful e-commerce website is an ongoing process that requires constant optimization and adaptation to changing market conditions and customer needs.

How to pick a Domain Name for your E-Commerce Website

Choosing a domain name for your e-commerce website can be a big deal because it can affect your brand, SEO, and overall success. Here are some things to keep in mind when choosing a domain name.

- **Keep it simple and easy to remember:** Pick a domain name that is short and easy to type and remember. Don't use spellings that are difficult to read or unfamiliar.

- **Make it easy to brand:** Your domain name should be

  unique and relevant to your brand. You can use your brand name or a keyword that matches your business.

- **Think about SEO:** Your domain name should include keywords that describe your product or service. This can help search engines rank your website higher.

- **Avoid already trademarked names:** Ensure your domain name doesn't violate any existing trademarks or copyrights.

- **Choose a domain extension:** Think about the different options, such as .com, .net, .org, etc. The most common and well-known extension is ".com," but many other options may be better for your business.

- **Check if it's available:** Before choosing a domain name, ensure it's not already taken. Use a domain name registrar to find out if the name you want is available and to buy it.

How to Put Yourself Out There

Before choosing a domain name for your e-commerce website, take your time and do some research. It's a big choice that can affect your online presence.

Adding New Products to your Online Store

If you want to add items to your online store, you usually have to do the following:

1. **Sign in to the administration area of your online shop**

To proceed with this stage, you must have access to the backend

of your online store. Here, you can modify your store's products, orders, and other settings. To accomplish this, you will normally need to use your username and password to log in to the administration panel of your online store.

2. **Navigate to the "Products" or "Inventory" section to view your products or inventory**

You should be able to get to your store's "Products" or "Inventory" section from the main dashboard or menu once you have successfully logged in to your account. You can manage the products in your store here, including adding new ones, modifying existing ones, and removing existing ones.

3. **Click the "Add Product" button to add a product**

You should see an "Add Product" or "New Product" button under the "Products" or "Inventory" menu. When you click this button, a new page or form will open where you can input the information about the product you are listing.

4. **Complete the following product information**

The product information that you are required to submit could be different based on the platform and your business settings, but it usually comprises the following details:

- **Product name:** This is the name of your product, which needs to be understandable and descriptive.

- **Product description:** A detailed explanation of your products, including a list of their features and benefits and any other information to help customers make informed decisions about their purchases.

- **Product price:** The price of your product, which should be determined based on your costs, the demand of the market, and the level of competition in the market.

- **Product image:** Include high-quality images of your product. They must present your product in the best form possible. Customers will have an easier time visualizing the product, which will pique their interest in the item.

- **Product variations:** If your product is available in various sizes, colors, or other variants, the information you provide should probably include this information.

How to Put Yourself Out There

- **SKU:** This means stock-keeping unit, and it is a unique identifier that can help you keep tabs on your sales and inventory levels.

- **Product tags:** Relevant keywords or phrases that, when used in a search or filtering system, can help customers find your products.

You may be required to specify other parameters, such as the product's visibility and availability, depending on the platform and settings of your store. You may, for instance, wish to make the product visible to all customers, or you may wish to limit its visibility to registered customers only. You could also want to select an availability status for the product, such as "in stock" or "out of stock."

5. **Save or Publish**

Once you have entered all required product information, you can save it by clicking the "Save" or "Publish" button. The first option allows you to save the product for future use just in case you need to make some edits before the listing goes live. Once you publish the listing, customers can view your product on your online store and also make purchases.

Adding products to your online store is a simple process. However, it is essential to take the time to give customers accurate and detailed product information to help them make informed purchasing decisions. You can improve customer satisfaction, increase sales, and establish a loyal customer base for your online store if you implement what I mentioned.

Here are a few tips to keep in mind when listing products in your online store:

- Customers will be able to understand the products better and make informed decisions about what to buy if you use clear and attractive photos and descriptions for your products.

- If you want to make it easier for customers to navigate your store, you should think about categorizing or organizing products that are quite similar to one another.

- Using SEO (search engine optimization) strategies on your product pages will help improve their visibility in search results, which will help increase organic traffic to your online store. This may include adding relevant keywords in the titles and descriptions of your product listing and optimizing the photos and metadata associated with those products.

- Always check and update your product listings to ensure they have the most up-to-date and correct information. This can help improve customer trust and satisfaction and help you discover opportunities to improve the product offerings over time.

Equipping Yourself with the Necessary Software Tools

How to Put Yourself Out There

You can run your online business successfully with the help of a wide range of e-commerce solutions. E-commerce tools are software programs like platforms, apps, and plug-ins that help store owners manage their online shops. Although there are many different types of ecommerce tools, they all serve the same function: to speed up, organize, and automate the processes involved in operating and growing an online store. Consider some of the following sorts of e-commerce tools as some of the most essential ones:

- **Platforms for e-commerce**

If you're just starting out, you can build your online business on an e-commerce platform instead of launching your own website. E-commerce platforms allow you to build, improve, and maintain an online storefront for your business. Amazon, Shopify, WooCommerce, Magento, and BigCommerce are a few examples of well-known e-commerce platforms.

- **Payment gateway**

A payment gateway is a piece of software that enables businesses to accept financial transactions over the internet. This allows you to connect your online store safely to payment processors like PayPal and Stripe.

- **Shopping cart software**

Customers can explore your online store, add products to their cart, and check out with the help of shopping cart software. Any e-commerce business shouldn't neglect it as a tool because it provides customers a convenient online shopping experience and helps you increase sales.

- **Inventory management**

An inventory management tool helps you keep track of your products so that you don't run out of stock or overstock. It can also ensure you always have the right products available by helping you optimize your stock levels.

- **Shipping and fulfillment**

This tool helps you manage your shipping processes, such as printing shipping labels, tracking items, and processing returns; ShipStation, Shippo, and Easyship are three popular options.

- **Customer relationship management (CRM)**

This refers to software that helps you manage your interactions with customers. This could include monitoring customer information, sending out marketing emails, and handling customer service issues. Salesforce, HubSpot, and Zoho CRM are three prominent options.

- **Marketing tools**

Marketing tools can help you promote your online store and get more people to visit your website. Facebook Ads and email marketing tools like MailChimp and Klaviyo are all popular options. Google Analytics is one of the most commonly used solutions.

How to Put Yourself Out There

- **Social media management**

Every online business should have a social media marketing strategy for organic traffic. A social media management tool can help you track how many people engage with your posts and schedule updates for multiple platforms.

- **Customer review**

If you want to build trust and credibility with potential clients, you need to have reviews from happy customers. With the help of a customer review tool, it's easy to get customer reviews and put them on your website.

- **Analytics**

Analytics tools can help you keep track of your website visitors,

sales performance, and where you can make improvements. Google Analytics, Optimizely, and Kissmetrics are good options to use.

These are just a few examples of the different kinds of e-commerce tools that you may need to run your online business successfully.

Creating Visibility (Getting your First Clients)

There's no sugarcoating it – getting the first clients for your online store can be tough. You've worked hard to get your business off the ground, but now you need to find ways to get people to see and buy from your store. The good news is that you can do a few things to increase visibility and attract customers.

1. **Search Engine Optimization (SEO)**

One of the most effective ways to create visibility for your online store is through SEO (search engine optimization). SEO is all about optimizing your online store, products, and content to make sure it ranks highly on search engines. By ensuring that you use relevant keywords in your content and product descriptions and optimizing your site for mobile devices, you can increase the chances of people finding your store when they search online.

2. **Content Marketing**

Content marketing requires you to produce valuable and engaging content while also being relevant to the audience you are trying to reach. This type of content includes blog posts, videos, infographics, and social media posts. Spreading this content across your website and various social media channels will help you bring in new potential customers and raise awareness for your brand.

3. **Social media promotions**

How to Put Yourself Out There

Social media is another great way to create visibility for your online store. Having a presence on platforms like Facebook and Instagram allows you to reach a wide audience and get potential customers interested in what you have to offer. Try posting regular content related to your store and engaging with customers by responding promptly to comments and messages. You can also use social media ads to target specific audiences and get even more eyes on your store

4. **Email marketing**

Email marketing involves compiling a list of email subscribers who have expressed an interest in purchasing your products. You should regularly contact them with exclusive offers, product updates, and newsletters to keep them interested in your business.

5. **Influencer Marketing**

This involves forming partnerships with individuals who command a sizable following on social media platforms. They can raise awareness for your business by promoting your products to their audience.

6. **Pay-per-click (PPC) advertising**

If you want more people to visit your website, you should try using pay-per-click (PPC) advertising. You can use Google Ads and other advertising platforms to accomplish this goal.

Finally, consider partnering with other businesses to increase visibility for your online store. Look for companies that offer services or products complementary to yours and consider partnering with them to create joint marketing campaigns. This will allow you to tap into their existing customer base and get more customers interested in what you have to offer.

By increasing visibility for your online store, you can ensure that more people are aware of your business and start shopping with you. With some creativity, you can find different ways to get your store seen, land your first customers, and boost your sales.

Always remember that consistency and persistence are the two most important factors in determining whether your marketing approach will be successful.

Copywriting: An Important Tool

Marketing a product or service online can be done using a wide variety of strategies and approaches, all of which go under the umbrella term known as online or digital marketing.

Successful online business owners know there is more to digital marketing than simply putting up a website, shelling out money for PPC campaigns, employing SEO, and/or providing exceptional products and services to people who shop online. Copywriting is one of the most powerful tools you have at your disposal to sell your business idea successfully.

How to Put Yourself Out There

Copywriting is an essential component of digital marketing, becoming more widely used. Copywriting is any form of writing done to sell a product or service for a business. Copywriting is used across various mediums, including websites, social media platforms, commercials, and brochures, to encourage a specific audience to perform a desired action.

You won't have to be the one selling your products and services yourself if you hire the skills of excellent digital copywriting, which can address the demands and needs of your audience and offer your products and services. Here are a few arguments supporting your decision to use the skills involved in copywriting.

1. **It distinguishes your business's marketing from the rest**

Copywriting is not just about constructing sentences in English and publishing them online. Effective copywriting is about appealing to the feelings of your audience and working to pique their interest. An excellent piece of copywriting will leave the readers wanting more and wondering how your business might help them or solve their problems or challenges.

The tone of voice of a well-written copy should unify the values, aspirations, problems, and solutions associated with your business. This will allow for more effective communication with your audience. A good copywriting piece will evoke feelings and spark interest, boosting customers' awareness of your online business.

2. **It is beneficial for SEO**

High-quality content is one of the most important criteria that Google considers when ranking websites. Websites that score highly on search engines feature content that is unique, comprehensive, and presented in a long form. Your website has the potential to quickly move up in the search engine rankings and get more visitors if the copywriting on it is done correctly. As soon as you have great content, you can add keywords related to your business and for what your audience is searching.

3. It enhances the user's overall experience

An excellently written copy can still be personalized content helpful and relevant to the target audience. The fact that this content fosters trust and loyalty in your business is the primary reason for its enormous influence on your readers.

An excellent strategy to become an authority in your industry is to use all skills that an excellent digital copywriting piece can offer to produce informative and engaging content for your

audience.

A lot of businesses hire copywriters to create content for their websites. Some choose the "Do It Yourself" (DIY) method. In any case, you have to keep the following in mind when creating your content:

- Get to know your target audience and figure out their problem and challenges.

- Make the title of your content attention-grabbing and interesting.

- Use "power" words – words that trigger a psychological or emotional response. These are persuasive and irresistible words.

- Ensure your content is engaging, interesting, and easy to read and understand.

- Establish a connection with your audience and retain their interest.

- End your content with an irresistible call-to-action.

A great copy will drive your conversion and skyrocket your sales.

How to Establish your Reputation

In this digital age, when everything is done online, you need to

build a good online reputation. Even though it takes time and effort to establish a positive online presence, all it takes is a few negative reviews or bad press to ruin it. Many businesses have discovered that they have little control over what is written about them on digital platforms. However, they have learned that they can improve their image if and when anything hurts their online reputation by paying attention to customer feedback and addressing problems head-on.

The following are some methods you can use to build your reputation online:

1. **Offer high-quality product**

Sell only high-quality products. If your customers notice that you sell only authentic products, they will trust your brand and become loyal customers. They will not only become repeat buyers but also your brand ambassadors who promote your brand and recommend your products to others.

2. **Offer excellent customer service**

One of the best ways to build a good online reputation is to offer excellent customer service. This includes but is not limited to quickly and nicely answering their questions, complaints, and feedback from customers.

3. **Build a strong social media presence**

Use social media platforms to connect with your audience and build a strong online presence. Regularly post good content and respond quickly to comments and messages.

4. **Encourage customer reviews and testimonials**

Ask satisfied customers to leave reviews and testimonials on your website, social media profiles, and other relevant platforms. Reviews and testimonials from happy customers can help people trust and believe in your business.

5. **Build relationships with influential people**

Work with influential people in your field to promote your products or services. This can help people recognize and trust your brand.

6. **Create valuable content**

Make sure your content is high-quality and relevant to your audience. This can include blog posts, videos, podcasts, and other content that shows your expertise and gives value to your audience.

7. **Monitor your online reputation**

Search for your business name, products, and services on search engines and social media sites regularly to monitor your online reputation. Respond quickly to any bad reviews or comments.

By using these strategies, you can build a good online reputation that will help you get new customers, retain existing ones, and grow your business.

The Power of Networking

Business networking is making and keeping connections with other professionals within and outside of your industry so that you can benefit from each other. Attending industry conferences and engaging with colleagues on social media are examples of networking.

Networking can have a positive impact on your business. Building relationships with people in your business area can help you discover new ideas, find cooperation possibilities, and become a thought leader. Networking requires strategy and intention. This involves choosing essential people and organizations to connect with, crafting a clear message about your abilities and interests, and reaching out to others.

Here are a few networking tips to consider:

1. **Establish goals:** Determine your networking goals and create a plan to achieve them.

2. **Attend industry events:** Industry events are great places to meet new people and learn about industry trends.

3. **Associations:** Online forums and local gatherings provide professional networking opportunities.

4. **Utilize social media:** LinkedIn and other platforms can help you network and promote yourself.

5. **Follow up:** After meeting someone new, send a unique message or email to maintain the relationship.

6. **Offer assistance:** Offer support when appropriate and if you have the necessary skillset. This will make your contact trust your expertise and view you as reliable.

7. **Ask for help at the right time:** Once your connections have become a part of your network, don't be afraid to ask for help if needed. They are more likely to offer you a helping hand.

Knowing how to use business networking successfully can help your business grow by saving you time and reducing stress. Networking can help you generate business leads, learn industry standards, identify key trends, increase brand awareness, understand different perspectives, receive mentorship, and build confidence.

Branding: A Crucial Part of Online Businesses

Having a strong brand identity is essential for any online business. Your brand represents who you are and what you stand for and delivers an important message to potential customers. It's easy to see why having a unique and memorable brand is so important.

Creating an effective brand identity isn't always straightforward, but it's worth the effort. A cohesive and well-designed logo, website, social media presence, and even packaging can all help you stand out from the competition. It's also essential to ensure that your branding is consistent across all platforms. When customers see your brand, they should instantly recognize it as yours.

Your branding can also reflect the core values of your business and appeal to potential customers. While designing a logo or website might seem intimidating, plenty of affordable tools and services help you create an effective brand identity for your online business. Even if you don't have the budget for a professional designer, there are several free resources to help you get started on creating your unique and memorable brand.

Finally, it's important to remember that branding is ongoing work. As your business grows and evolves, so should your brand identity. Constantly reviewing and refining your branding will ensure customers stay engaged and your brand stays fresh. With the right branding strategy, you can ensure that your online business stands out from the crowd.

Here are some branding tips you can use for your online business:

- Develop a unique logo that captures the essence of your business. It should be easily recognizable and stand out in a crowd.

- Design an attractive website that showcases your brand. Make sure it is easy to navigate and contains all the necessary information.

- Make sure your branding is consistent across all platforms, including social media, email marketing campaigns, and any other forms of communication you use.

How to Put Yourself Out There

- Be aware of current trends in design and take advantage of them whenever possible.

- Stay focused on what makes your business unique so that your brand stands out.

- Don't be afraid to experiment with different ideas for branding, and always review and refine your approach as needed.

- Ensure that you deliver a message that speaks to potential customers and reflects the core values of your business.

Creating an effective brand identity is key for any successful online business. With the right strategy, you can ensure your brand stands out from the competition and appeals to potential customers. The key is to focus on what makes your business unique, design an attractive website and logo, and remain consistent across all platforms. With a little bit of work and creativity, you can create an unforgettable brand identity for your online business.

If you still need help, there are a huge number of resources available online to help you create an effective brand identity for your business. You can find tools and services that make logo design easier or tips on creating a website. There is also lots of advice out there on how to use social media as part of your branding strategy.

With the right tools and guidance, you can build a strong brand identity for your online business to help it stand out from the competition and appeal to your target customers.

Key takeaways

- Know the best way to launch your e-commerce platform or create your own website. The former is a better option for beginners.

- Equip yourself with the necessary software tools to help you manage and run your online business more efficiently.

- Work on creating visibility for your new business by getting your first clients, starting with those in your network.

- Use copywriting to great effect as a tool in marketing and promotion.

- Establish a good reputation by delivering quality services or products consistently.

- Networking is essential to help you find new opportunities, build relationships, and grow your reach.

How to Put Yourself Out There

- Branding is crucial to online businesses; create an effective brand strategy for maximum visibility and success.

In the next chapter, we will look at various marketing strategies to help you build a profitable online business.

CHAPTER 6

Marketing: Driving Growth and Sales

Welcome to the exciting world of marketing. In today's digital age, businesses have an unprecedented opportunity to reach out to customers and drive growth through online channels. You've come a long way in this book, learning how to build your online business. It's time to learn how to create effective marketing strategies for your online business that can boost your sales and revenue.

Marketing is all about identifying your target audience, understanding their needs and preferences, and compellingly communicating the value of your products or services to them. Whether you're just starting out or an established business looking to grow, a solid marketing plan is essential for success.

In this chapter, we'll guide you through developing a marketing strategy tailored to your online business. From understanding your target market to choosing the right channels and messaging, we'll cover everything you need to know to drive growth and sales.

So, get ready to learn some valuable insights and practical tips that you can apply to your online business today. Let's dive in!

The Power of SEO

Marketing is one of the most crucial elements of any online business. Your business can reach its target audience through marketing, generating leads, and ultimately driving sales. Without effective marketing, an online business will unlikely succeed in a highly competitive digital landscape. In this chapter, I will discuss how to develop various marketing strategies for your profitable online business.

But first, let us dive into the most fundamental of these strategies, SEO, and how you can use it to drive growth and sales for your online business.

But what exactly is SEO?

Search Engine Optimization (SEO) is the process of making your website better to rank higher in search engine results pages (SERPs). When someone searches the internet for a keyword or phrase on search engines like Google, Bing, etc., the search engine returns a list of relevant web pages in the SERPs. The order in which these web pages are listed is based on several factors, including the relevance and quality of the content on the page, the website's authority and popularity, and the user's location and search history.

So, why is SEO that important?

SEO is essential for every online business because it is the most

cost-effective way to drive organic traffic to your website. Organic traffic is visitors who find your website through search engines rather than paid advertising or social media. When your website ranks higher in the SERPs, users are likelier to click on it, leading to increased traffic to your business, leads, and sales. Research shows that the first page of Google captures 71% of search traffic clicks, and the top five results on the first-page account for 67% of all clicks. That's why a lot of businesses invest so much in SEO.

So How Do You Get Started with SEO to Grow Your Online Business?

Though the concept seemed self-explanatory when I was first introduced to SEO, the application was yet overwhelming, the technicalities, terminologies, and all. But after much reading, extensive research on the subject, and implementing it in my online businesses, I got cleared.

SEO can initially seem overwhelming, but it's a reasonably straightforward process. Here are steps to help you get started with SEO:

1. **Do keyword research:** This identifies the words and phrases that your target audience type in the search bar when searching for similar products or services. You can start by brainstorming a list of keywords relevant to your business. Then, use popular tools like Google Keyword

Marketing: Driving Growth and Sales

Planner, SEMrush, and Ahrefs to identify related keywords and estimate their search volume and other important SEO metrics to discover the possibility of that keyword ranking

high on SERPs.

2. **Optimize your website:** Once you have identified your main target keywords, you need to optimize your website content to include these keywords in strategic locations, such as the title tag, meta description, header tags, and body text. Use your keywords naturally and avoid "keyword stuffing," which can hurt your rankings. Keyword stuffing is the practice of filling keywords or numbers into web pages to manipulate rankings in Google Search results. These keywords usually appear unnaturally or out of context in a list or group.

3. **Build high-quality backlinks:** These are links pointing from other websites to your website. They are an essential ranking factor in Google's algorithm and can help to improve your website's authority and popularity. Building high-quality backlinks requires outreach to other websites for a mention, creating valuable content that other websites can use and link back to your site as a source, and networking with other site owners for a link exchange.

4. **Improve your website's user experience:** Google values websites that provide a positive user experience. This means having a website that loads quickly, is easy to

navigate, and offers high-quality content relevant to your target audience.

5. **Monitor and analyze your results:** SEO is an ongoing process. Monitoring and analyzing your results is essential. It will help you to identify areas of your strategy that are working well and areas that need improvement.

In addition to these steps, staying up-to-date with the latest SEO best practices and algorithm updates is essential. This can involve reading industry blogs and attending conferences and webinars. By staying informed and continually optimizing your strategy, you can maximize your chances of success and drive growth and sales for your online business.

Can You Do SEO Yourself, or Should You Hire Professionals?

Whether to do SEO or hire professionals depends on your experience and resources. While it is possible to do SEO yourself, it can be time-consuming and complex. SEO also requires significant knowledge and expertise to get results. If you have the time, willingness to learn, and resources to dedicate to SEO, you can handle it independently.

However, hiring SEO professionals may be more effective if you are short on time or lack the necessary expertise. SEO agencies and consultants have the experience, knowledge, and tools to develop and execute effective SEO strategies. They can help you identify the best keywords to target, optimize

Marketing: Driving Growth and Sales

your website, build high-quality backlinks, and monitor and analyze your results.

When choosing an SEO professional, it's essential to do your research and choose a reputable and experienced provider. Look for SEO professionals with a proven track record of success, positive client reviews, and a focus on white-hat SEO practices that comply with Google's guidelines.

Freelancers vs. SEO Agency

Whether to hire a freelancer or an SEO agency depends on your needs and resources. Here are factors to consider when making your decision:

1. **Expertise**: SEO agencies typically have a larger team of experts with diverse skills and experience, while freelancers often specialize in one area. If you have a complex SEO strategy that requires a range of skills, an agency may be a better fit. A freelancer may be a good choice if you need help with a specific task or project –keyword research, SEO content writing, and building backlinks.

2. **Resources**: SEO agencies generally have access to more resources, such as advanced tools and software, than individual freelancers. An agency may be better if you need advanced analytics or devices to track your SEO performance.

3. **Communication**: Freelancers often offer more personalized and direct contact, while agencies may have a

more formal and structured communication process. A freelancer may be better if you prefer to work closely with an individual and have direct access to them. An agency may be better if you prefer a more structured and organized approach.

4. **Cost**: Freelancers generally charge lower rates than agencies but may not have the same expertise or resources. Agencies may be more expensive but offer more comprehensive

   services and higher expertise.

So, consider your budget, the complexity of your SEO strategy, and your communication preferences when deciding whether to hire a freelancer or agency for your SEO need. Researching and choosing a reputable and experienced professional, whether you choose a freelancer or an agency, is also essential.

The Magic of Web Push Notifications

Web push notifications are clickable messages sent from a website to a user's web browser. They appear in a small pop-up window, typically in the corner of the screen, and are designed to capture a user's attention and prompt them to take action.

Marketing: Driving Growth and Sales

In online marketing, web push notifications are used to engage with website visitors and keep them informed about new content, special offers, and other updates. They can be personalized and targeted based on a user's behavior on the website, such as the pages they visited or the products they viewed.

Web push notifications are an invaluable marketing tool because they are delivered directly to a user's browser without requiring them to provide an email address or other personal information. This means businesses can reach their target audience more efficiently and immediately than traditional email marketing.

To receive web push notifications, users must first opt-in by clicking on a prompt that appears when they visit a website.

Once they have opted in, they can manage their notification settings, including choosing which websites they receive notifications from and what messages they want to see.

How to Create an Effective Web Push Notification Strategy

Creating an effective web push strategy involves understanding your audience, crafting compelling messages, and optimizing your approach over time. Here are some critical steps to follow:

1. **Define your audience:** Who are you trying to target with your web push notifications? What are their interests and

behaviors? Use audience segmentation to tailor your messages to specific groups.

2. **Craft compelling messages:** Your notifications should be concise, engaging, and personalized. Use action-oriented language and clear calls-to-action to encourage users to click through your website.

3. **Timing is key:** Consider when your audience will likely be online and engaged with your content. Schedule your notifications for optimal times to increase the chances of users seeing and clicking on them.

4. **Optimize your approach:** Use A/B testing to try out different messaging and timing strategies and track your metrics to see what's working and what's not. Use this information to refine your approach and improve your results over time.

5. **Respect user preferences:** Give users the option to opt out or adjust their notification settings, and be mindful of how frequently you send notifications. Overusing web push notifications can make users opt out or get annoyed, and this can hurt your brand reputation.

An effective web push strategy involves understanding your audience, crafting personalized and engaging messages, as well as testing and refining your approach based on user feedback and data analysis.

Marketing: Driving Growth and Sales

Users' On-Site Activities to Apply Actionable Web Push and How to Implement Them

There are several on-site activities that you can use to apply actionable web push notifications. Here are a few examples:

1. **Abandoned cart reminders:** If a user adds items to their cart but doesn't complete the purchase, you can send a web push notification reminding them of their abandoned cart and offering a discount or other incentive to complete the purchase.

2. **Product recommendations:** You can use data on a user's browsing and purchasing history to send personalized product recommendations via web push notifications, encouraging them to return to the website and purchase.

3. **Event reminders:** If you are hosting an event, you can use web push notifications to remind your visitors to register or attend and provide details about the event.

4. **Limited-time offers:** You can use web push notifications to announce limited-time sales or promotions, encouraging your visitors to take advantage of the offer before it expires.

To implement these on-site activities, you need a web push notification tool that integrates with your website and allows you to send targeted, personalized messages to users. It would also help to clearly understand your audience and their preferences so that you can tailor your messages, making them relevant and engaging.

Examples of practical web push notification tools

There are several web push notification tools available that you can use to send targeted and compelling messages to your audience. Here are a few examples:

1. **OneSignal:** This popular web push notification tool offers features such as audience segmentation, personalized messaging, and A/B testing. It integrates with a variety of platforms, including WordPress and Shopify.

2. **PushEngage:** This web push notification tool offers advanced targeting and personalization options, automation, and drip campaigns. It integrates with popular website builders like Wix, WordPress, and Shopify.

3. **Pusher:** This web push notification tool offers real-time notifications, audience segmentation, and advanced reporting and analytics. It also offers integrations with popular platforms such as WordPress and Magento.

4. **WebEngage:** This is a comprehensive marketing automation platform that includes web push notifications, email marketing, SMS marketing, and more. It offers advanced targeting and personalization options, automation, and reporting features.

5. **VWO Engage:** This web push notification tool offers targeted messaging, segmentation, and A/B testing

features. It also integrates with popular platforms such as Shopify and WooCommerce.

These are just a few examples of the many web push notification tools available. Consider your specific needs and budget when choosing any options and the features and integrations offered.

Email Marketing: Turning Visitors into Buyers

Email marketing is an effective form of digital marketing that involves sending promotional messages or newsletters to a list of subscribers via email. Email marketing aims to build relationships with subscribers, increase brand awareness, and drive sales.

Here are some practical ways to use email marketing to grow your online business:

1. **Build a targeted email list:** The first step to a successful email marketing campaign is building a list of subscribers interested in your product or service. You can do this by offering incentives such as free content or exclusive discounts to encourage people to sign up for your email list so they can always receive your messages for future offers or discounts.

2. **Personalize your emails:** When you send personalized emails, you'll have a higher open rate and click-through rate than generic emails. Use subscriber data to personalize your emails, including their name, interests, and past purchases.

3. **Segment your email list:** Split your email list into smaller segments based on subscriber behavior, demographics, or interests. This allows you to send targeted emails that are more relevant to each subscriber, increasing the chances of conversion.

4. **Use attention-grabbing subject lines:** Your subject line is the first thing subscribers see when they receive your email. Use attention-grabbing subject lines that encourage your subscribers to open your email and read it.

5. **Create engaging content:** Your email content should be interesting, informative, and relevant to your subscribers. Use high-resolution images, videos, and infographics to make your emails more visually appealing.

6. **Include a clear call-to-action:** Your email should have a clear call-to-action that encourages your subscribers to act, such as visiting your website or purchasing.

7. **Test and optimize:** Test different forms and elements of your email campaigns, including subject lines, content, and strategic calls to action, to see what works best for your audience. Use the results to optimize your email marketing strategy and improve your ROI.

Marketing: Driving Growth and Sales

By following these tips, you can use email marketing to grow your online business and build long-lasting relationships with your subscribers.

How to Set Up Email Marketing Campaigns That Convert

Use the steps below to create a conversion-drive email marketing campaign:

1. **Define your goals:** Before starting your email marketing campaign, defining your goals is essential. What do you want to achieve? Is it to increase sales, generate leads, or promote a new product or service? Your goals will shape the content and structure of your campaign.

2. **Build your email list:** Create a list of loyal subscribers who have opted in to receive your emails. You can build your email list through lead magnets, such as free guides or discount codes, or by placing a sign-up form on your website or social media channels.

3. **Segment your email list:** Segment your email list based on behavior, interests, or past purchases. This allows you to send targeted and relevant emails to each subscriber, increasing your conversation rate.

4. **Choose your email marketing platform:** Choose an email marketing platform that fits your needs and budget. Popular options include Mailchimp, Constant Contact, ConvertKit, Aweber, and ClickFunnels.

5. **Create your email content**: Create compelling content that aligns with your goals and target audience. This includes a strong subject line, personalized content, a clear call-to-action, and social proof.

6. **Design your email template:** Use a visually appealing one that reflects your brand and content. Make sure your email is mobile-responsive and easy to read.

7. **Test and optimize your email:** Before sending it to your entire list. And this includes checking for grammar and spelling errors, ensuring links work correctly, and testing different subject lines and content to see what works best.

8. **Send your email:** Schedule your email at the optimal time for your target audience. Monitor the performance of your email and adjust as needed.

9. **Follow up with subscribers:** Follow up with subscribers who have shown interest but have not purchased. And this can include sending a follow-up email with additional incentives or offering a personalized consultation.

With these steps, you can create an effective email marketing campaign that converts and helps you achieve your business goals.

Other Strategies to Promote Your Online Business

Marketing: Driving Growth and Sales

Besides SEO, web push notifications, and email marketing, there are many practical strategies to promote your online business. These include:

1. **Content marketing:** Create valuable and engaging content, such as SEO articles, blog posts, videos, and infographics, to attract and retain a target audience.

2. **Social media marketing:** Leverage social media platforms, such as Facebook, Instagram, and Twitter, to build a following and engage with customers. Post valuable content regularly to keep your customers engaged and well-informed about your product, service, and industry trends.

3. **Pay-per-click (PPC) advertising:** Use targeted ads on search engines and social media platforms to drive traffic and conversions.

4. **Influencer marketing:** You can collaborate with social media influencers who can help you promote your products or services to their followers.

5. **Affiliate marketing:** Partner with other businesses or individuals to promote your products or services and share revenue.

6. **Referral marketing:** Encourage your customers to refer friends and family to your business in exchange for incentives.

7. **Webinars:** You can host webinars or online events to educate and engage with your audience. This is a great way to showcase your brand.

8. **Podcasts:** Start a podcast to share your expertise and build a loyal following.

9. **Online directories:** List your business on online directories such as Yelp, Google My Business, and Yellow Pages.

10. **Guest blogging**: Write guest posts for other websites to build backlinks and increase brand exposure.

11. **Online reviews:** Encourage satisfied customers to leave positive reviews on platforms like Google, Yelp, and TripAdvisor.

12. **User-generated content:** Encourage your customers to create and share content related to your brand, such as reviews, social media posts, and photos.

13. **Online contests and giveaways:** You can also host contests or giveaways to generate buzz and engagement.

14. **Chatbots:** Use chatbots to provide personalized customer service and support.

15. **Video marketing:** Use videos to showcase your products or services and connect with your audience. You can start a Vlog on YouTube and share educative videos with your

audience.

16. **Virtual reality (VR) and augmented reality (AR):** Use VR and AR technologies that create immersive experiences for your customers.

17. **SMS marketing:** Use text messaging to send promotions and alerts to customers.

18. **Voice search optimization:** You can also Optimize your website and content for voice search to stay ahead of the curve.

19. **Online marketplaces:** Sell your products or services on websites like Amazon, eBay, and Etsy.

20. **Podcast advertising:** Use podcast advertising to reach a targeted audience and increase brand exposure.

To implement these strategies, identify which ones align with your business goals and target audience, create a plan and budget for each process, and track your results to determine what works best for your business. Remember to stay up-to-date with the latest trends and technologies to stay ahead of the competition.

Content vs. Social Media vs. Email Marketing

Content, social media, and email marketing are essential to a comprehensive digital marketing strategy. Each of these channels has unique strengths and weaknesses, and their effectiveness depends on the specific goals and audience of the campaign.

Here is a comparison of content marketing, social media marketing, and email marketing in terms of conversion, ROI, reach, CTR, and other metrics based on the latest empirical data and verifiable statistics:

1. **Conversion**

    - **Content marketing:** According to HubSpot, content marketing strategies generate three times as many leads and conversions as traditional outbound marketing, and content marketing conversion rates are six times higher than other methods.

    - **Social media marketing:** The average conversion rate for social media advertising is 1.5%, according to WordStream.

    - **Email marketing:** The average conversion rate for email marketing campaigns is around 4%, according to Smart Insights. This can, however, vary widely depending on the industry and type of campaign.

2. **ROI**

    - **Content marketing:** According to the Content Marketing Institute, content marketing only generates

Marketing: Driving Growth and Sales

three times as many leads and conversions as traditional outbound marketing but costs 62% less.

- **Social media marketing**: According to Hootsuite, the average ROI for social media advertising is around 95%.

- **Email marketing:** According to Campaign Monitor, email marketing has an average ROI of 4200%.

3. Reach

- **Content marketing:** Content marketing can reach a broad audience through search engines, social media, and other online channels. However, building an audience and establishing authority in a particular niche can take a lot of time.

- **Social media marketing:** Social media marketing can reach a large and diverse audience, but it is increasingly pay-to-play, and organic reach is declining.

- **Email marketing:** Email marketing has a high potential reach if the email list is targeted and high-quality. However, the reach can be limited if the emails end up in the spam folder or are not opened at all.

4. CTR

- **Content marketing:** The average click-through rate for content marketing is around 0.5%, according to Smart Insights.

- **Social media marketing:** The average click-through rate for Facebook ads is 0.90%, according to WordStream. However, this can vary depending on the targeting and ad creative.

- **Email marketing:** The average click-through rate for email campaigns is around 2.5%, according to Campaign Monitor. However, this can vary depending on the quality of the email list, the subject line, and the email content.

Here's a comparison table of content marketing, social media marketing, and email marketing based on various metrics:

Metric	Content Marketing	Social Media Marketing	Email Marketing
Conversion Rate	6x higher than other methods (HubSpot)	Average of 1.5% for social media advertising (WordStream)	Average of 4% for email campaigns (Smart Insights)
ROI	Costs 62% less than traditional outbound marketing (Content Marketing Institute)	Average ROI of around 95% for social media advertising (Hootsuite)	Average ROI of 4200% (Campaign Monitor)

Marketing: Driving Growth and Sales

Reach	Wide reach through search engines, social media, and online channels	Large and diverse audience, but increasingly pay-to-play	High potential reach if the email list is high-quality and targeted
CTR	Average of 0.5% (Smart Insights)	Average of 0.90% for Facebook ads (WordStream)	Average of 2.5% for email campaigns (Campaign Monitor)

It's important to note that these metrics are not the only factors to consider when evaluating the effectiveness of these channels and that the point of each channel may vary depending on the specific goals and audience of the campaign.

Overall, each of these channels has its strengths and weaknesses, and their effectiveness will depend on the specific goals and audience of the campaign. Content marketing is effective for building authority and trust. Social media marketing effectively reaches a broad audience and builds brand awareness. And email marketing is effective for nurturing leads and driving conversions. The key to success is to use these channels together in a coordinated and strategic way to maximize their impact on your business.

Understanding Time-Sensitive Promotions

This strategy can effectively drive more sales for your online business by creating a sense of urgency and encouraging customers to act quickly. Here are some strategies for running time-sensitive promotions:

1. **Flash sales:** Offer a huge discount on a product or service for a short period, such as 24 hours. This can create an instant sense of urgency and encourage customers to purchase quickly.

2. **Limited-time offers** A discount or promotion is only available for a limited period, such as a weekend or a week.

3. **Countdown timers:** Use a countdown timer on your website or email campaigns to create an instant sense of urgency and encourage customers to purchase before the timer runs out.

4. **Early bird discounts**: Offer a discount to customers who purchase a product or service before a specific date or time. This can encourage customers to act quickly and incentivize them to buy before the offer expires.

5. **Free shipping:** Offer free shipping for a limited time or when a customer's order reaches a certain amount, such as a weekend or a week for orders above $100, respectively. This can encourage customers to purchase and take advantage of the free shipping offer before it expires.

6. **Bundle deals:** Offer a special deal for purchasing a bundle

Marketing: Driving Growth and Sales

of products or services for a limited time. This can encourage customers to buy and take advantage of the bundle deal before it expires.

7. **Limited quantity offers:** Offer a promotion or discount only for a limited number of products or services. This can create an instant sense of urgency and encourage customers to purchase quickly before the offer expires or the product sells out.

Here are some popular examples and case studies of time-sensitive promotions you can learn from:

5. **Amazon Prime Day:** Amazon's annual 2-day event offers exclusive discounts and deals for Prime members for a limited time. The event has become extremely popular and has helped drive sales for the company.

6. **Nordstrom Anniversary Sale:** Nordstrom's annual sale offers discounts on new fall merchandise for a limited time. The deal is highly anticipated by customers and has become a popular event for the company.

7. **Domino's Pizza:** Domino's Pizza has run several successful time-sensitive promotions, including offering half-off all pizzas ordered online for a limited time. These promotions have helped drive sales and increase customer engagement.

8. **Airbnb:** Airbnb has run several time-sensitive promotions, including offering a $50 credit to customers who referred a friend and a 25% discount on bookings made for a specific

time. These promotions have helped drive new customer acquisition and increase bookings.

9. **Starbucks Happy Hour:** Starbucks runs a regular "Happy Hour" promotion that offers a discount on select drinks for a limited time. This promotion has helped drive traffic to stores and increase sales during slow periods.

10. **Zulily:** Zulily is an e-commerce site that offers daily product deals for women, children, and the home. The site's time-sensitive promotions include daily contracts that expire after a certain period and "flash sales" that offer huge discounts for a short period.

When running time-sensitive promotions, it's essential to communicate the promotion's terms and expiration date to customers and ensure your website and checkout process can handle the increased traffic and sales volume. You should also track the results of your promotions to evaluate their effectiveness and adjust your strategy as needed.

Developing a Winning Online Marketing Strategy

As you have seen in previous sections, you can market your online business using various methods. Of course, there is SEO, content marketing, email marketing, social media marketing, and the list goes on. Each strategy reflects a specialty and a unique set of skills and best practices. This

Marketing: Driving Growth and Sales

implies that SEO is very different from content marketing or any other digital marketing strategy. Therefore, developing a digital marketing strategy is not an easy task. However, I'm going to guide you on addressing the basics, and here's how you can develop a winning marketing strategy:

1. **Define your target audience:** Identify the characteristics of your ideal customer, including demographics, interests, and pain points. Use this information to then create buyer personas that represent your target audience.

2. **Set your business goals:** Define your business goals, such as increasing website traffic, generating leads, or driving sales. Ensure your goals are specific, measurable, relevant, and time-bound (SMART).

3. **Conduct a competitive analysis:** Research your competitors and analyze their online marketing strategies, including their strengths and weaknesses. Identify specific areas where you can differentiate yourself and develop a unique value proposition.

4. **Choose your online marketing channels:** Identify the online marketing channels most relevant to your target audience and business goals. This may include search engine optimization (SEO), email marketing, pay-per-click (PPC) advertising, content marketing, social media marketing, or influencer marketing.

5. **Develop a content strategy:** Create a rich content strategy that aligns with your business goals and target

audience. This may include creating blog posts, videos, infographics, social media posts, email newsletters, or other types of content.

6. **Create a budget:** Determine and allocate your online marketing budget to the most effective channels and campaigns. Ensure that your budget is realistic and allows for testing and optimization.

7. **Set KPIs and track your results:** Define key performance indicators (KPIs) that align with your business goals, such as website traffic, leads generated, or sales. Use analytics tools to track your results and adjust your strategies as needed to improve your performance.

8. **Test and optimize:** Continuously test and optimize your online marketing strategies to improve your results over time. Use A/B testing, analytics data, and feedback from your audience to refine your strategy and achieve better outcomes.

By implementing these steps, you can develop a winning online marketing strategy that helps you reach your target audience, achieve your business goals, and grow your business over time.

Customer Relations is Key to Your Success

Marketing: Driving Growth and Sales

Effective customer relations are crucial to the success of any online business. Building and maintaining solid relationships with your customers can help increase customer loyalty, drive repeat business, and attract new customers through positive word-of-mouth. In today's highly competitive online marketplace, providing exceptional customer service and support is no longer a luxury; it's a necessity.

In online business, customers don't have the opportunity to interact physically with your products or services before they make a purchase. This can create a sense of uncertainty or mistrust, making it even more important to establish a relationship of trust with your customers. Effective customer relations can help you build this trust by showing your customers that you value them, understand their needs and concerns, and are committed to providing them with a positive experience.

Additionally, unhappy customers can write negative reviews and feedback, spreading quickly online and damaging your brand's reputation. By establishing strong customer relations, you can ensure customer satisfaction, mitigate negative reviews, and address customer concerns promptly and effectively. This can help turn dissatisfied customers into loyal advocates for your business.

Overall, customer relations are essential for building a successful online business. By focusing on providing exceptional customer service and support, you can create a loyal customer base that will help drive the growth and success of your business.

Here are some ways to analyze and improve your customer relations:

1. **Communication:** Communication is the key to building and maintaining customer relationships. Ensure that you are communicating with your customers in a timely, clear, and consistent manner. Provide multiple communication channels, such as email, phone, live chat, and social media, to make it easy for customers to contact you.

2. **Personalization:** Personalization can help you build stronger customer relationships. Use data and analytics to segment your customer base and provide personalized recommendations, offers, and content. Address customers by name and use their past purchase history and preferences to create a more customized experience.

3. **Feedback:** Encourage and use customer feedback to improve your products, services, and customer experience. To collect feedback, provide easy-to-use feedback channels, such as surveys, reviews, and social media polls. Use this feedback to identify areas for improvement and address customer concerns.

4. **Responsiveness:** Respond promptly to customer inquiries, concerns, and complaints. Show your customers you care about their experience by addressing their problems promptly and effectively. Use automated email

Marketing: Driving Growth and Sales

and chatbots to respond quickly even outside business hours.

5. **Loyalty programs:** Implement loyalty programs to reward customers for their patronage and incentivize repeat purchases. Offer exclusive discounts, early access to new products, or other perks to keep your customers engaged and loyal to your brand.

6. **Social media engagement:** Engage with your customers on social media to build relationships and improve your brand image. Respond to comments and messages promptly, share user-generated content, and run social media contests and giveaways to keep your customers engaged.

7. **Continuous improvement:** Continuously analyze and improve your customer relations strategies. Use customer satisfaction surveys and metrics, such as Net Promoter Score (NPS), to track your performance and identify areas for improvement. Use this data to refine your customer relations strategies and enhance your customer's experience with your business.

Start paying attention to what your clients are saying and take steps to eliminate any issues that lead to dissatisfaction. It takes work to create a successful customer relations and retention campaign. Always putting the customer's needs first and exceeding their expectations is the first step in creating a meaningful customer experience. If you do that, your customer relations will significantly improve, drive loyalty and trust, and the effect will be reflected in your sales and business growth.

Key takeaways

- Leverage the power of SEO to drive more organic search traffic and better rankings in SERPs.

- Give web push notifications a try to reach customers on their devices as soon as they visit your website.

- Utilize email marketing campaigns to turn visitors into buyers by creating personalized and engaging content.

- Maximize the effectiveness of your online marketing efforts by combining strategies such as content, social media, and email marketing.

- Take advantage of time-sensitive promotions to increase engagement and conversions.

- Follow best practices for developing a winning online marketing strategy for your business.

Marketing: Driving Growth and Sales

- Remember that customer relations are the most important part of any marketing strategy, which drives loyalty and trust.

- In the next chapter, we'll discuss online value proposition as an effective marketing strategy for increased sales and improved customer satisfaction.

Chapter Seven

Value Proposition for Improved Profits

Having a strong online value proposition is essential to staying ahead of the competition and attracting customers. So, what exactly is a value proposition? Simply put, it's the unique combination of benefits and value that your business offers to customers. It sets you apart from your competitors and gives customers a reason to choose your products or services over others.

But how can you effectively communicate your value proposition online? That's where this chapter comes in. We'll explore the different elements of a strong online value proposition, including clear messaging, customer-focused language, and unique selling points.

It's not just about making a quick sale. A strong value proposition also leads to improved customer satisfaction and loyalty. By clearly communicating your value to customers, you can build trust and establish long-term relationships that benefit your business and customers.

So, whether you're a small business owner or a marketing

professional, this chapter will provide valuable insights and strategies for improving your online value proposition and achieving increased sales and customer satisfaction. Let's get started!

Understanding Online Value Proposition (OVP)

An Online Value Proposition (OVP) is a statement that tells the customer or visitor to an online business about the unique solution it provides. It is a promise that a business makes to its target audience regarding the benefits that its customers will enjoy from interacting with the business by purchasing products or services.

A well-written OVP should be easy to understand. It should be clear, concise, and simple. When writing an OVP, use language the target audience can easily understand and connect with to communicate the key benefits of your business's products and services. In addition, a powerful OVP needs to be consistent across all marketing channels, such as the website, social media, and email marketing campaigns.

Creating an OVP is a continuous process. Even after writing one, it needs to be continually tested and improved. Businesses can ensure their OVP remains effective and relevant over time by regularly reviewing customer data and feedback and changing their promises and benefits.

In the end, a strong online value proposition (OVP) is a key part of any successful online business. It helps communicate the benefits that set a business apart from its competitors in a saturated market, and it contributes to effectively communicating that value.

Why your Business Needs an Online Value Proposition

In today's highly competitive online marketplace, an online value proposition (OVP) is crucial for businesses that want to thrive. It is a clear and concise statement that expresses a business's unique solutions to its target audience. Here are some reasons why your business needs an OVP:

- A well-crafted OVP can help your business stand out and be remembered. With so many businesses vying for customers' attention, having a clear and easy-to-understand OVP can help customers understand why they should choose your brand over others.

- A strong OVP can help you connect with your target audience by addressing their needs and wants. By modifying your OVP to relate to your customers, you can develop a relationship with them and grow a loyal customer base that is more likely to continue to do business with you.

- A compelling unique selling proposition (USP) can encourage customers to take action, such as making a purchase, subscribing, or sharing. A clear and concise OVP that presents your business's solutions can attract

Value Proposition for Improved Profits

customers to the call-to-action button and increase conversion rates.

- A strong OVP can establish your business as an authority in your field, improving your reputation and building customer trust.

- An OVP can ensure that your marketing and communication strategies are clear and organized, helping your business maintain its focus on its mission and goals. Consistency in messaging across all channels and touchpoints is essential.

- A flexible OVP can be adapted to various formats, allowing you to engage with your customers across multiple touchpoints, such as social media, email marketing, and your website.

In conclusion, a well-crafted OVP should be a top priority for every business that wants to succeed online. It can help your business stand out, connect with your target audience, increase conversions, establish credibility, maintain focus, and stay flexible. By dedicating time and resources to creating the best OVP for your target audience, you can position your business for success in the ever-changing digital landscape.

Creating a Killer Value Proposition for Your Business

As we have established above, every online business needs an online value proposition. Now, let me show you how to create an effective OVP for your business. To create an OVP for your

website, you must:

1. **Identify your target audience:** Know your target audience and their needs, preferences, and habits. It is crucial to clearly grasp who your target audience is and what they need to create an effective OVP. You can use this information to develop a more tailored, relevant OVP that speaks directly to their needs.

2. **Define your unique selling proposition (USP):** Your business's unique selling proposition (USP) is what differentiates it from other brands in the market or makes it unique. It could be your pricing strategy, the quality of the products you sell, the great customer service you provide, or any other factors that set your business apart from the competition.

3. **Focus on the benefits**: Instead of focusing only on the product features, you should emphasize the benefits your customers will get from using your products. These may include benefits such as lower overall prices, more convenience, user-friendliness, or improved customer service.

4. **Keep it short and clear:** Your online value proposition (OVP) should be clear, concise, and easy to understand. Avoid jargon, complicated terms, and long paragraphs if you don't want your audience to get confused.

Value Proposition for Improved Profits

5. **Use of graphics and multimedia:** Using visuals and multimedia in your OVP is a great way to make it more engaging and memorable for your customers. Think about using pictures, videos, infographics, and other visual materials to communicate your point more clearly.

6. **Test and refine:** After creating your OVP, let your target audience see it and get their feedback so you can make changes if necessary. Use this feedback to improve your online value proposition (OVP) until it speaks to your target audience and tells them what your business is about.

It is important to keep in mind that a strong OVP should be engaging and drive conversions. Therefore, you should prioritize creating a captivating OVP that speaks directly to your target audience and helps you stand out in a crowded digital marketplace as soon as possible.

Improving Your Product's Value: Enhancing Your Offer

The perceived benefits or worth a product gives its users is referred to as product value. It is determined by the level of satisfaction or usage a consumer obtains from a product in relation to its cost. A product's value can be determined by various factors, including its quality, functionality, design, features, branding, packaging, and customer service. A product that serves a high value to its consumers is more likely to have a competitive advantage in the market and attract a loyal customer base ready to pay a premium.

Here are the major factors that determine a product's value:

- **Absolute value:** The absolute value of a product is how well it meets the needs and expectations of its target customers.

- **Comparative value:** A product's comparative value can be defined as how effectively it satisfies the needs and wants of its customer base compared to other similar products currently available on the market.

- With that said, here are a few things worth knowing about product value:

- **Product value is subjective:** The value that a customer places on a product is a matter of opinion and might vary from person to person. It's possible that what is important to one customer won't be to another. While developing a product, it is crucial to have a solid understanding of its intended market and the requirements of that market.

- **Product value is not determined by price:** A product's value is not solely determined by its price but plays a significant role. Consumers are willing to pay a higher price for products that offer greater benefits or provide a better solution to their problems than those that do not.

- **Product value can be enhanced through features and benefits:** Products with more added features and benefits

Value Proposition for Improved Profits

typically have a higher perceived worth. These attributes can include things like simplicity (how easy they are to use), durability (how long they last), reliability (how reliable they are), convenience (how convenient they are), and -

adjustment (how much room there is for modification).

- **Brand reputation can impact product value:** A brand's reputation can affect the product value; consumers frequently connect the worth of a product to the reputation of the brand that offers it. There is a correlation between a positive brand reputation and an increased ability to command a greater perceived value for the products the brand sells.

- **Product value can change over time:** How people think about a product's value can change over time as the market changes and as people's tastes change. Consequently, it is very important to always observe your products and make changes to both their features and their benefits to keep increasing their value proposition.

You can produce or sell products that not only satisfy the needs and expectations of their target audience but also lead to higher levels of customer satisfaction and loyalty when you have a thorough understanding of what customers value in a product.

Effective Ways to improve your Product's Value

In today's competitive marketplace, it's essential for businesses to continually focus on improving the value of their products to stay relevant and meet the evolving needs of their customers. While some may think that improving the value of a product requires drastic changes or a complete overhaul, there are many effective ways to enhance its value without breaking the bank. From refining your product's features to optimizing its packaging, there are numerous strategies that businesses can use to enhance their products' value and boost their competitiveness. In this response, we will explore some effective ways to improve your product's value, helping you stand out in the marketplace and meet your customers' demands.

- **Do market research:** Market research helps you understand your target market's needs, expectations, and problems or challenges. With this information, you can find ways to improve your product's value and make it stand out from the competition.

- **Improve the quality:** Improving the quality of your product can help it stand out in the market and make it look more valuable. Quality can mean the materials used, the manufacturing process, or the product's performance.

- **Enhance its features:** Customers will value your product more if you add new features or improve the ones you already have. This may involve adding new technology, simplifying the user interface, or improving the product's functionality.

Value Proposition for Improved Profits

- **Offer great customer service:** Providing excellent customer service can increase customer loyalty and satisfaction, which in turn can increase the perceived value of your product.

- **Offer customization:** Customization options allow customers to tailor the product to their specific needs and preferences, thereby increasing its value.

- Create bundles: Putting together product bundles that provide your customers with a complete solution to their needs can make them think your product is worth more. Bundles may include complementary products, accessories, or services.

- **Simplify the user experience:** Simplifying the user experience can make your product more user-friendly and enhance its value to customers. This can include simplifying the user interface, giving clearer instructions, or providing online tutorials.

- **Create a sense of exclusivity:** Creating a sense of exclusivity around your product can increase its perceived value. This can be achieved through limited edition products or by offering exclusive access to certain features or benefits.

- **Provide education:** Providing education and resources to your customers can increase the value of your product by helping them get the most out of it. This can include offering online tutorials, user guides, or webinars.

- **Collaborate with Influencers:** Partnering with influencers can help increase brand recognition and credibility, which in turn can increase the perceived value of your product. Influencers can help promote your product to their followers and provide valuable feedback.

- **Emphasize sustainability:** Focusing on sustainability can increase your product's perceived value for environmentally conscious customers. This can include using sustainable materials, reducing waste, or implementing environmentally friendly manufacturing processes.

- **Offer competitive pricing:** Offering competitive pricing can increase the perceived value of your product by making it more attractive compared to similar products on the market. This can be achieved through pricing strategies such as discounts, sales, or price matching.

- **Designing a better product:** Improving a product's design can increase its value regardless of its main selling factor. Conduct market research to find out how people feel about an existing product's design and improve it.

- **Reward high-performers**: Rewarding high-performers increases product value. A public ranking system and prizes for product mastery can boost consumer loyalty and recognition. Leaderboards are one way to recognize high-performing products.

- **Invest in attractive packaging:** Give a better impression of the product's worth with attractive packaging. It can provide a long-lasting impression that a product's value is high by using high-quality materials, colors, images, and writing that appeal to its target audience.

Improving the value of your product is a continuous process that requires a deep understanding of your customer's needs and expectations. By implementing the strategies discussed above, you can enhance your product's overall value without breaking the bank. Remember to regularly gather feedback from your customers and use it to update your product development and improvement efforts. By prioritizing the value of your product, you can increase customer loyalty and satisfaction, ultimately leading to increased sales and business success.

Success Factors of OVPs

An Online Value Proposition (OVP) is critical to any digital marketing strategy. It represents a business's unique value to its customers through its online presence, and it plays a significant role in driving customer engagement and loyalty. The success of an OVP relies on several factors, including clarity, relevance, and differentiation. A clear and relevant OVP can help businesses stand out in a crowded online marketplace, while a differentiated OVP can help establish a competitive advantage. Let's explore the key success factors of online value propositions and provide you with insights into how you can create and communicate a compelling OVP that resonates with your target audience.

An effective value proposition involves three critical areas that need to be addressed to create a compelling statement:

1. **Identify a specific problem that is being faced by a target audience**

It's crucial to understand the unique challenges that your target audience is experiencing to create a value proposition that resonates with them. By identifying their specific pain points, you can create a message that speaks directly to their needs.

Crafting an effective value proposition that resonates with your target audience is crucial for your business's success. However, it's unrealistic to expect a single positioning statement to speak to everyone. Therefore, the first step in creating a compelling value proposition is identifying your core target audience. Whether you're speaking to entrepreneurs, professionals, or moms, each group may share a similar need, but their desired solution may vary drastically.

Once you've identified your audience, your next step is to state the problem you're solving for them succinctly. Some audiences may already know their problem, while others may only recognize the signs.

Value Proposition for Improved Profits

Articulating the problem you solve in writing conveys to your target audience that you understand their needs and have the perfect solution to their pain points. Clearly stating what your solution does enables you to push interested prospects further down the marketing funnel.

When potential customers read your value proposition statement, they can self-identify if the product is the right fit for them before even contacting you. The result is that you spend more time talking to interested buyers that have already self-identified. This approach can improve your sales efficiency and help you sell faster.

2. **Articulate how your product or service solves the identified problem**

Once you've identified the problem, you need to explain how your product or service can solve it. This means clearly articulating the benefits and features of your products in a way that is easy to understand and relatable to your target audience.

Merely stating the problem you're solving for your target audience is not enough; you must also provide a clear understanding of how you solve their problem. This is where a well-crafted value proposition can make all the difference.

Unfortunately, many businesses use their value proposition as an opportunity to brag about their product or list every feature they offer. This approach is unnecessary and can be a major turnoff for potential customers.

Instead, your product or service description should be an opportunity to illustrate to your target audience that you understand their needs and empathize with their specific problem. You should provide context that explains how each feature or benefit you offer can help uniquely solve their problem.

3. Communicate the audience-specific intangible and quantifiable benefits of your solution

Your value proposition should also highlight the benefits of your solution in a way that is both tangible and intangible. Quantifiable benefits, such as increased efficiency or cost savings, can be measured and easily understood. Intangible

benefits, such as improved customer satisfaction or brand reputation, may be more challenging to quantify but are still important to communicate to your audience.

If you're operating in a competitive industry, it's likely that your competitors have comparable products or services available. To stand out in the market, you need a strong value proposition that highlights the benefits and values of your product's features. This approach will enable you to differentiate yourself from the competition and establish your brand as the go-to option for potential customers.

Combining these elements results in a powerful and straightforward statement that provides your target audience with a clear understanding of your offer and why they should care about it. Let's explore each of these components in more

Value Proposition for Improved Profits

detail to create a value proposition that resonates with your target audience and sets your business apart from the competition.

Example of an Effective Value Proposition

One example of an effective online value proposition is the one used by Dropbox, the cloud-based storage provider. Their value proposition consists of a headline that reads, "Get to your files from anywhere, on any device." A sub-headline reinforces this: "Share and collaborate on your work with others in real-time." The unique value proposition is "Safely and securely store and share your files with Dropbox." The supporting points include features such as syncing across devices, automatic backups, and file sharing.

Visuals are used to illustrate how Dropbox works and how it can be used in various situations. Social proof is provided in the form of testimonials from satisfied customers. Finally, the call to action is a simple "Sign up for free" button that encourages users to try out the service. Dropbox's value proposition effectively communicates its product's key benefits and unique value while providing clear calls to action that encourages customer engagement.

Key Techniques for Managing OVPs

Managing an online value proposition involves an ongoing effort to ensure your messaging and offerings align with customer needs and wants. Here are some key techniques for managing online value propositions:

1. **Keep abreast with your industry trends:** Keeping up with industry trends helps your business stay ahead of the competition and adjust to changes in customer behavior. By following industry thought leaders and attending relevant conferences, your business can gain insights into emerging trends so you can adjust your online value proposition accordingly.

2. **Monitor what your competitors are offering:** Keeping an eye on competitor offerings can be done by regularly monitoring their websites, social media, and marketing campaigns. You can use this information to identify new opportunities or threats and adjust your online value proposition accordingly.

4. **Analyze website and campaign data:** By tracking website and campaign data, you can gain insights into customer behavior and identify areas for improvement in the online value proposition. For example, if a website has a high bounce rate, this might be an indication that you need to adjust your messaging or user experience.

5. **Continuously improve your website design and user experience:** Website design and user experience are critical components of the online value proposition. Regularly optimizing the website design and user

experience can improve engagement and higher conversion rates.

6. **Build a strong brand:** A strong brand is essential to a successful online value proposition. Building a strong brand involves consistent messaging, branding, and visual identity across all channels, including the website, social media, and advertising campaigns.

7. **Check and respond to customer feedback:** Customer feedback provides valuable knowledge about what they like and dislike about your product or service. Monitoring and responding to customer feedback can help you improve your online value proposition and build customer loyalty.

10 of the Best E-Commerce Value Propositions

In no particular order, these are the best E-Commerce platforms that use a good value proposition in their various niches to stand out from their competition. You can learn a thing or two from them.

1. **Amazon**

Tagline: "Spend less. Smile more"

What do they sell: Everything.

Online Value Proposition: Amazon has built its reputation on offering consumers an extensive selection of products. Their value proposition is all about convenience and choice, as customers can easily find and purchase almost anything they need through Amazon's platform.

2. Zappos

Tagline: "Free shipping and free returns"

What they sell: Shoes, sneakers, boots, and clothing.

Online Value Proposition: Zappos has built its brand on excellent customer service, and its value proposition reflects this by focusing on providing a hassle-free shopping experience. By offering free shipping and returns, Zappos removes the risk for customers and makes it easy for them to try out new products.

3. Apple

Tagline: "Think Different"

What they sell: Apple designs, manufactures, and markets smartphones, personal computers, tablets, wearables, and accessories. They also sell a range of related services. The Company's products include iPhone, Mac, iPad, AirPods, Apple TV, Apple Watch, Beats products, HomePod, iPod touch, and accessories.

Value Proposition for Improved Profits

Online Value Proposition: Apple has always been known for its sleek, modern design and cutting-edge technology. Their value proposition emphasizes this by positioning Apple products as the best and most innovative on the market.

4. Warby Parker

Tagline: "We've got your eyes covered"

What they sell: Warby Parker offers high-quality eyeglasses, sunglasses, contacts, and eye examinations at an affordable price.

Online Value Proposition: Warby Parker disrupted the traditional eyewear industry by offering designer glasses at a lower price point than competitors. Their value proposition is all about providing high-quality, stylish eyewear accessible to everyone.

5. Dollar Shave Club

Tagline: "Shave time. Shave money"

What they sell: It delivers razor blades monthly and offers additional grooming products for home delivery.

Online Value Proposition: Dollar Shave Club's value proposition is centered on affordability and convenience. By offering a subscription service for razor blades, they make it easy and affordable for customers always to have a fresh, sharp razor.

6. **Etsy**

Tagline: "Shop for handmade, custom, and unique gifts"

What they sell: It is primarily used for selling vintage items, handmade goods, art, and crafts.

Online Value Proposition: Etsy's value proposition is all about providing a marketplace for unique, handmade items that can't be found elsewhere. This appeals to customers who are looking for unique products and want to support small businesses and artisans.

7. **Airbnb**

Tagline: "Belong anywhere"

What they sell: Airbnb is an online marketplace connecting people who want to rent out their homes with people looking for accommodations in specific locations.

Online Value Proposition: Airbnb's value proposition is centered on providing a unique travel experience. By offering local homes and neighborhoods as accommodations, Airbnb allows travelers to immerse themselves in the local culture and have a more authentic travel experience.

8. **Blue Apron**

Tagline: "We're building a better food system"

Value Proposition for Improved Profits

What they sell: Blue Apron is an online store offering kitchen tools, pantry staples, packaged meal kits, and wine bundles.

Online Value Proposition: Blue Apron's value proposition is all about providing fresh, high-quality ingredients and easy-to-follow recipes for home cooking. This appeals to customers who want to eat healthy, homemade meals but don't have the time or knowledge to shop for ingredients and create recipes on their own.

9. Casper

Tagline: "No More Sleepless Nights"

What they sell: In addition to mattresses, the company also sells bed frames, pillows, bedding, a weighted blanket, a dog bed, and accessories like a mattress topper.

Online Value Proposition: Casper's value proposition is centered around providing a comfortable, high-quality mattress tailored to each customer's needs. By offering a range of mattress options and a 100-night trial period, Casper makes it easy for customers to find the perfect mattress for their unique needs.

10. Birchbox

Tagline: "Meet your best friend in beauty"

What they sell: An online monthly subscription service that sends its subscribers a box of products including makeup, other beauty products, skincare items, perfumes, organic-based products, and various other cosmetics.

Online Value Proposition: Birchbox's value proposition is about personalization and discovery. By offering a subscription service that sends personalized beauty samples to customers each month, Birchbox allows customers to try out new products and discover their favorites without committing to full-sized products.

Key takeaways

- Understand how online value propositions (OVPs) work and why your business needs one to succeed.

- Create an impressive, killer value proposition to make customers notice your product or service.

- Enhance your offer by improving your product's value.

- Keep an eye on success factors like understanding your target audience, meeting their needs and expectations, and effective communication to grow your business.

- Use key techniques discussed in this chapter to effectively manage your online value proposition.

Value Proposition for Improved Profits

- Learn how the top 10 e-commerce websites use their value propositions to attract customers and implement them in your business.

- Implement the insights from this book chapter to maximize profits and gain a competitive edge in the marketplace.

- In the next chapter, I'll reveal more tips to keep your business afloat and expand the business when due.

Chapter Eight

Staying in Business

Running a successful business is no easy feat and takes more than just a great idea and a lot of hard work. The key to staying afloat and thriving in today's fast-paced and ever-changing online business landscape is to be adaptable, innovative, and always willing to learn.

In this chapter, I'll share some valuable tips and strategies that you can use to keep your business on track and grow it to its fullest potential.

We'll cover everything from analyzing performance and knowing when to expand or change products, monitoring KPIs, backend sales, and upselling to retaining and satisfying your customers.

So, sit back, grab a cup of coffee, and get ready to learn valuable insights on staying in business and thriving in today's competitive market.

Analyzing Your Performance

You have your online business up and running. To further

consolidate your milestones and successes, now's the time to critically examine your performance metrics.

E-commerce site performance analysis evaluates how well a website is performing in terms of speed, functionality, user experience, and other metrics. It involves analyzing various aspects of the site, including its load times, responsiveness, and overall user experience, to identify areas for improvement and optimize its performance.

You have exclusive access to a wealth of data on customer behavior and trends on your website. By analyzing this data, you can make informed decisions that lead to growth and customer satisfaction.

One of the key metrics to track is your site traffic. Analyzing website traffic lets you see which pages are most popular and which are not getting enough attention. You can use this information to optimize the website for better user experience and engagement.

Another important metric is the conversion rate. This measures the percentage of visitors who make a purchase. Analyzing conversion rates can help businesses identify areas where the purchasing process could be improved, such as checkout processes or product descriptions.

You can also track customer satisfaction through surveys and feedback forms. You can use this information to improve the customer experience and address any issues that arise.

Analyzing sales data can provide insights into which products

Staying in Business

are selling well and which are not. This information can be used to make product development and inventory management decisions.

Social media analytics can also be valuable for online businesses. By tracking engagement metrics such as likes, shares, and comments, you can see which content resonates with your audience and adjust your social media strategy accordingly.

Overall, comprehensive online business analytics can provide invaluable insights into customer behavior and trends. By using this information to make informed decisions, you can continue to grow and satisfy your customers.

In terms of sales, here are some ways to analyze and understand your online sales for greater performance:

1. **Customer lifecycle:** Understanding the customer lifecycle and journey is crucial to your business's success. By analyzing the different stages of the customer lifecycle, you can identify areas where you can improve customer experience and drive sales. For example, if you see a high drop-off rate during the checkout process, you may want to investigate whether the process is too complicated or if technical issues need to be addressed.

2. **Engagement metrics:** Measuring engagement metrics such as reach, impressions, and engagement is important for assessing the effectiveness of your marketing efforts. These metrics can help you understand how well your

content resonates with your target audience and adjust your marketing strategy accordingly. For example, if you see high engagement rates on social media but low engagement rates on email campaigns, you may want to focus on social media to drive more traffic and sales.

3. **Cost of engagement:** Understanding the cost of acquiring each customer ensures you get the best value for your money. By analyzing the cost per lead and cost of acquiring a customer, you can determine which marketing channels are the most effective and adjust your strategy accordingly. For example, if you see a high cost per lead for a particular advertising channel, you may want to consider reducing your spending on that channel and focusing on other channels driving better results with less spending.

4. **User conversion:** The conversion rate is a critical metric for any business because it measures the effectiveness of the sales process. By analyzing the conversion rate, you can identify areas to improve your customer experience and drive more sales. For example, if you see a high cart abandonment rate, you may want to investigate whether there are technical issues or if the checkout process is too complicated for customers.

5. **Customer retention:** Customer retention is important for any business because retaining existing customers is less expensive than acquiring new ones. By analyzing customer lifetime value, average customer lifespan, average purchase value, total revenue, and the number of purchases, you can

identify areas where you can improve customer loyalty and drive repeat sales. For example, if you see a high churn rate, you may want to investigate whether product or customer service issues need addressing.

Analyzing these metrics is essential for understanding online sales performance and making data-driven decisions that can drive growth and success. By leveraging tools such as Google Analytics, you can gain valuable insights into customer behavior and use that information to optimize your website, marketing campaigns, and sales process for better performance.

Knowing When to Expand or Change Products

Expanding your products is key to maintaining financial stability and success in your business, while ignoring business growth can result in falling behind or suffering losses due to competition. Generally, business expansion entails additional effort, such as hiring more staff or securing more funding. Product expansion is when a company creates a new product in the same product line as an existing brand.

Benefits

In the ever-changing business landscape, it is essential to constantly evaluate your product offerings and determine when to expand or change them. Here are some reasons why this is important for business growth:

- **Staying Relevant:** markets change over time, and what was

    popular yesterday may not be popular tomorrow. By expanding or changing your product offerings, you can stay relevant and appeal to changing customer needs and preferences.

- **Diversifying revenue streams:** By expanding your product offerings, you can diversify your revenue streams and reduce your dependence on a single product or market. This can help you weather downturns in specific markets and ensure long-term business sustainability.

- **Increasing customer value:** Offering new products can increase the overall value that you provide to your customers, making them more likely to remain loyal and refer others to your business.

- **Capitalizing on new opportunities:** Expanding your product offerings can also help you capitalize on new opportunities that arise in your market. For example, if you notice a gap in the market that you can fill with a new product, this can help you gain a competitive advantage.

- **Addressing customer feedback:** By listening to customer feedback, you can identify areas where your product offerings may fall short. By changing or expanding

Staying in Business

your offerings to address these gaps, you can improve customer satisfaction and loyalty.

Overall, knowing when to expand or change your product offerings is crucial for staying competitive and growing your business over time. By staying flexible and adapting to changing market conditions and customer needs, you can set yourself up for long-term success.

Making the decision

Deciding whether to expand your product line or change your product offerings in your online business can be a critical decision that requires careful consideration. Here are some factors to consider when making this decision:

- **Market demand:** It's important to understand the market demand for your current and potential new products. Look at industry trends and consumer behavior to determine if there is a demand for new or different products in your niche.

- **Customer feedback:** Your customers are your best source of feedback. Listen to their feedback and evaluate their purchasing behavior to see if they are interested in new or different products.

- **Competitive landscape**: Analyze your competition and their product offerings. Are they offering products that you're not? Are they offering products that you are but with better features, pricing, or quality? Knowing your competition's strengths and weaknesses can help you make informed decisions about your product line.

- **Profitability:** Evaluate the profitability of your current product line and potential new products. Consider factors such as production costs, shipping and fulfillment costs,

   marketing expenses, and potential revenue.

- **Brand identity:** Consider whether new products align with your brand identity and overall business strategy. If you have a well-established brand with a specific target audience, adding products that don't align with your brand could confuse or alienate your current customers.

- **Resources:** Think about the resources needed to expand your product line or change your products. Do you have the financial, operational, and logistical resources to handle the change?

Ultimately, the decision to expand your product line or change your products will depend on your unique situation and business goals. By carefully considering these factors and conducting thorough research, you can make an informed decision to benefit your business in the long term.

Monitoring Your KPIs

Staying in Business

Key performance indicators (KPIs) tracking provides deeper insights into a business's inner workings. Businesses that track their activities and metrics have a key advantage over their competitors. Working with dynamic key performance indicators (KPIs) empowers businesses to monitor and enhance critical areas of their operations, ultimately accelerating commercial success. Without data, businesses risk operating in the dark when making informed decisions and formulating strategies. However, not all KPIs are created equal, and focusing on the most important ones is essential.

What is KPI Tracking?

It is a definitive process of monitoring the most relevant metrics for increased business success using modern KPI software. By measuring KPIs regularly and automatically, businesses can increase productivity and decrease costs. The right KPIs selected for various business areas can also help organize and visualize large datasets, unlocking additional value from organizational data while setting targets and measuring incremental success.

KPI tracking tools offer a powerful vessel for organizational growth and progress, providing businesses with greater intelligence and visual innovations such as KPI dashboards that streamline operations for success in the competitive digital landscape.

Key Performance Indicators (KPIs) can help organizations monitor various aspects of their operations. Some typical KPIs include:

- **Revenue:** measuring revenue trends, profitability, and customer acquisition.

- **Workforce metrics:** tracking employee turnover rates, productivity, and recruitment challenges.

- **Customer experience:** evaluating product or service quality and feedback from customers.

- **Marketing effectiveness:** assessing sales performance, brand awareness, and marketing ROI.

- **Operational efficiency:** analyzing process efficiency, team performance, and individual productivity.

How do you calculate a KPI

Calculating a KPI requires defining clear and specific goals from the outset. Focusing on the right KPI and designing it with a narrow scope is crucial. For example, a new business may be more interested in tracking new customer acquisition, while an established business may prioritize tracking price and profitability.

Web analytics tools, such as Google Analytics, are commonly used for tracking KPIs. While these tools can track a vast amount of data, sometimes the metric being tracked is intangible or subject to individual interpretation, especially when measuring customer satisfaction. In such cases, multiple

Staying in Business

KPIs may be required, but it's important not to get overwhelmed with too much data.

The presentation of KPIs is also crucial. Visual representations of complex data can provide deep insights and improve understanding. When dealing with multiple KPIs, presenting them in a clear and interactive manner can help avoid confusion and enhance comprehension.

However, KPIs require constant evaluation to remain relevant and focused on the most critical parts of the business. Regularly reviewing KPIs helps ensure they remain aligned with business goals and can help make an informed decision based on available data.

Managing and Monitoring KPIs: Achieving Success

The success of Key Performance Indicators (KPIs) largely depends on the framework and the interface used to measure them. Since different types of data require unique templates, choosing the appropriate measuring tools is crucial.

For instance, Google Analytics is a comprehensive platform ideal for monitoring website KPIs. It provides detailed data on critical metrics like conversion rates and returning visitors. However, businesses need to be cautious of vanity metrics, which can be misleading. For example, a growing number of visitors may not translate to success if they are not the right target audience.

In-depth on-site analytics tools on social media platforms like Twitter offer effective KPI measurement. These tools provide essential information about customer reach, acquisition, and brand awareness. Combined with other software, they can provide invaluable insights to businesses.

Overall, choosing the right KPIs and using appropriate measuring tools can provide businesses with valuable insights and help them achieve their goals.

Back End Sales and Upselling

Capitalizing on the back end and up-sell products is a powerful marketing strategy many businesses overlook. By offering customers complementary or upgraded products just before they complete their purchase, you can increase your profits significantly.

Backend products are those that you sell after the initial sale. On the other hand, up-selling is when you present customers with another product or two in a pop-up window that appears after they fill out your order form and hit the submit button. Since the window opens with a confirmation of the original order and a thank-you message, customers do not feel as though they are being bombarded with ads.

While many businesses focus all their time, money, and energy on drawing in first-time visitors, it is far more profitable to focus on cultivating relationships with current customers. First-time customers are always the most expensive to acquire,

Staying in Business

but existing customers are easier to sell to. If you provided them with good value, excellent customer service, and delivered on your promise, they are more likely to buy from you again and again.

Statistics show that about 36% of people who have bought from you before will most likely buy again if you have something similar to offer. This means your customer base is a goldmine you need to focus on. It is crucial to understand the lifetime value of your customers, as 20% of them will be responsible for 80% of your profits.

To make the most of these loyal customers, show appreciation and offer special incentives to encourage them to continue buying from you. Doing so can build stronger relationships with your customers and create a steady stream of repeat business.

20 Tips for Staying in Business

1. **Develop a clear business plan:** Create a comprehensive business plan that outlines your goals, strategies, and target audience. This plan will guide your business operations and help you stay on track.

2. **Choose a profitable niche**: Identify a niche that aligns with your skills and interests. Conduct thorough market research to determine the demand for your products/services.

3. **Build a user-friendly website:** Create a website that is easy to navigate and visually appealing. Make sure your website is well-optimized for mobile devices and has fast loading times.

4. **Establish a strong brand:** Develop a strong brand identity that resonates with your target audience. Use consistent branding across all your marketing channels and content to build brand recognition.

5. **Offer high-quality products/services:** Ensure that the products/services you offer are of high quality and provide value to your customers. This will help you build a loyal customer base.

6. **Provide excellent customer service:** Offer exceptional customer service to build a positive reputation and increase customer loyalty. Respond promptly to customer inquiries and resolve issues quickly.

7. **Use social media marketing**: Employ social media platforms to connect with your target audience and promote your products/services. Use a variety of content formats to engage your audience.

8. **Invest in search engine optimization:** Optimize your website and content for search engines to increase visibility and drive traffic to your website.

9. **Leverage email marketing:** Use email marketing to build customer relationships and promote your

Staying in Business

products/services. Offer exclusive promotions and discounts to your email subscribers.

10. **Video content:** Use video marketing to showcase your products/services and personally connect with your audience. Consider creating tutorial videos or product demonstrations. Also, do not neglect short video content.

11. **Offer free resources:** Use eBooks, webinars, or templates to build credibility and attract new customers.

12. **Monitor your competition:** Keep an eye on your competition to stay updated on industry trends and best practices. This will help you stay ahead of the competition.

13. **Expand your reach with affiliate marketing:** Use

    affiliate marketing to expand your reach and increase your customer base. Offer commissions to affiliates who promote your products/services.

14. **Engage in content marketing:** Use content marketing to provide value to your audience and establish yourself as an industry expert. Use a variety of content formats, such as blog posts, infographics, and podcasts.

15. **Use data analytics to track performance**: Use data analytics to track the performance of your website, social media, and marketing campaigns. This will help you make data-driven decisions and optimize your strategies.

16. **Stay updated on industry news:** Stay informed on industry news and updates to stay ahead of the curve by attending seminars and conferences and networking with other professionals in your industry.

17. **Offer excellent payment options:** You should provide various payment options to cater to your customer's preferences. Consider offering payment plans or installment options.

18. **Focus on retention:** Focus on retaining your loyal customers by offering loyalty programs or exclusive offers. Keeping existing customers is easier and more cost-effective than acquiring new ones.

19. **Excellent shipping and delivery options:** Offer fast and reliable shipping options to provide a positive customer experience. Consider offering free shipping or returns to

    incentivize customers to purchase.

20. **Be flexible:** Be flexible and receptive to change. Monitor industry trends and adapt your strategies as needed to remain competitive and meet the changing needs of your customers.

Retaining and Satisfying Your Customers

Staying in Business

In today's competitive business landscape, it's no longer enough to attract new customers – retaining and satisfying them is equally important. With the rise of social media and online reviews, customers have more power than ever to share their experiences and influence the purchasing decisions of others. Therefore, businesses must focus on providing exceptional customer service and creating positive experiences to keep their customers returning. In this context, here are some insights into some effective strategies businesses can use to retain and satisfy their customers, thereby increasing customer loyalty and driving long-term growth.

1. **Know your customer:** The first step to satisfying your online customers is understanding who they are, what they want, and how they shop. Invest time in market research, surveying your existing customers, and analyzing their behavior to gain insights into their needs.

2. **Offer quality products and services:** The quality of your products and services will directly impact your customers' satisfaction. Make sure your products and services are of high quality, meet customer expectations, and are delivered on time.

3. **Provide excellent customer service:** Providing excellent customer service is crucial for satisfying your online customers. Make sure you are responsive to their inquiries, complaints, and feedback. Responding promptly to your customer's concerns can help build their trust and loyalty.

4. **Ensure user-friendly website navigation:** Your website should be user-friendly, easy to navigate, and aesthetically appealing. Your customers should be able to find what they are looking for easily, and the buying process should be simple and straightforward.

5. **Ensure website security:** Customers want to feel safe when shopping online. Ensure your website is secure by implementing SSL (Secure Sockets Layer) encryption, regularly updating software, and complying with privacy and data protection regulations.

6. **Provide clear product information:** Customers want to know what they are buying. Make sure your product descriptions, images, and videos provide clear and accurate information about your products.

7. **Offer multiple payment options:** Provide your customers with multiple payment options, including credit cards, debit cards, PayPal, and other payment gateways to make the buying process more convenient.

8. **Provide transparent pricing:** Provide transparent pricing, including all fees and taxes, to avoid any surprises for your customers during checkout.

9. **Make shipping and delivery easy:** Offer your customers different shipping and delivery options, including free shipping and tracking services, to make the process more convenient and transparent.

Staying in Business

10. **Offer returns and refunds:** Offer a clear return and refund policy that is easy for your customers to understand and follow. Make the process easy for your customers to avoid any frustration or dissatisfaction.

11. **Personalized customer experience:** Personalization is key to building customer loyalty. Use customer data to offer personalized recommendations, discounts, and promotions based on their shopping history and behavior.

12. **Encourage customer feedback:** Encourage customer feedback, including product reviews and surveys, to gain insights into their preferences and needs. Use this feedback to improve your products and services and show customers that you value their opinions.

13. **Use social media to engage customers**: Social media is a powerful tool for engaging customers, building brand awareness, and driving sales. Use social media platforms to connect with your customers, share valuable content, and promote your products and services.

14. **Provide customer support across multi-channels:** Offer customer support across multiple channels, including email, chat, phone, and social media, to make it easy for your customers to reach you and get the help they need.

15. **Monitor customer experience metrics**: Monitor customer experience metrics, including customer satisfaction, net promoter score, and customer lifetime

value, to gain insights into how well you satisfy your customers and identify areas for improvement.

16. **Continuously improve customer experience:** Improve your customer experience by regularly analyzing customer feedback, identifying pain points, and implementing changes to your products, services, and processes.

17. **Build brand loyalty:** Build brand loyalty by offering loyalty programs, exclusive offers, and personalized promotions to reward loyal customers and incentivize repeat purchases.

18. **Focus on customer retention:** Focus on customer retention as much as customer acquisition. Satisfied customers are more likely to become repeat customers.

19. **Quick response time:** Customers expect quick responses to their inquiries, so it's important to have a prompt response time. This can include responding to emails and social media messages within a few hours and having customer service representatives available by phone during business hours.

20. **Upselling and cross-selling:** Offer customers complementary products or upgrades during the checkout process. This can increase the overall value of their order and improve their satisfaction with their purchase.

21. **Follow-up:** Follow up with customers after their purchase to ensure they're satisfied with their order and

offer any assistance if needed. This can include sending a follow-up email or survey to gather feedback.

22. **Reviews and testimonials:** Positive reviews and testimonials can go a long way in building trust with potential customers. Encourage satisfied customers to leave a review or testimonial on your website or social media pages.

Satisfying your customers requires a combination of strategies aimed at meeting their needs and providing exceptional customer service. By continuously monitoring customer experience metrics, analyzing feedback, and improving products, services, and processes, you can build brand loyalty and retain satisfied customers. The key is to focus on both customer acquisition and retention to build a loyal customer base that will drive sustainable business growth.

Key takeaways

- Keeping track of how your business is doing is essential for long-term success, so it pays to take the time to look into your KPIs.

- If you're meeting customer needs and staying current, there's no need to reinvent the wheel. However, if you spot a gap in the market that your business can fill or see new trends emerging, it may be time to change your product.

- Keeping up-to-date with key performance indicators (KPIs) will give you insight into your business's performance and allow you to make informed decisions.

- Make sure always to offer your customers options for related products that are of genuine use to them through back-end offers and upselling.

- It pays to know the ins and outs of your industry, stay on top of trends, and understand what sets you apart from the competition.

- Loyal customers are key to long-term success, so treat them well by offering great customer service and incentives such as discounts or loyalty rewards. Doing so will go a long way in helping your business stay afloat.

Conclusion

The Online Business Academy for Beginners is a comprehensive guide that offers a proven roadmap to start and build a profitable online business that generates $15,000 passive income months with the best operations in place. The book is divided into three parts, covering everything you need to know to get your online business up and running successfully.

Starting an online business can be a great way to achieve financial freedom and personal satisfaction, but it requires more than just enthusiasm. Extensive planning, market knowledge, strategic thinking, and the willingness to constantly educate yourself are all necessary for success. Various marketing strategies include social media marketing, SEO, content marketing, and email campaigns. Email marketing is still viable for creating rapport with customers and fostering loyalty.

It is also important to have financial resources to support your business's upkeep as you try to grow it. Ultimately, launching a successful online business requires hard work, dedication, commitment, and preparation – but the rewards can be great.

Conclusion

The bottom line is: starting an online business can be a rewarding experience, and it doesn't have to involve a lot of risk

or cost. While certain risks and costs are associated with any business, you can minimize them and create a successful online venture by doing your research, staying informed, planning ahead, and taking advantage of the marketing channels available.

There are various online business models; this book reveals how to choose the right one based on industry research, risk and reward evaluations, legal requirements, and a well-prepared business plan. Before launching a successful online business, I must stress the importance of understanding legal requirements such as tax regulations, copyright and trademark laws, shipping restrictions, and customer privacy.

This book also provides a detailed roadmap for managing financial aspects effectively. It highlights the importance of establishing a budget, using accounting or bookkeeping software to track your finances, seeking professional advice, exploring inventory management software, and outsourcing tasks to freelance workers so you can focus on other important aspects of your business. These strategies can help streamline operations, reduce costs, and improve profitability.

An online value proposition (OVP) is a statement that conveys the key benefits of a product or service to customers. It should be tailored to customer needs and expectations while providing a clear call to action. Effective OVPs are essential in today's digital world, as they help convey the value of a business's products and services to customers. Managing an OVP involves an ongoing effort to ensure the messaging aligns with customer needs and expectations. By leveraging these techniques, businesses can create an optimal online value proposition that resonates with customers, drives engagement, and leads to

higher conversion rates.

An effective online marketing strategy is essential for any business looking to succeed in the digital age. This involves defining a target audience, setting business goals, conducting competitive analysis, choosing relevant online marketing channels, developing a content strategy, creating a budget, setting KPIs and tracking results, and testing and optimizing strategies. Additionally, customer relations are paramount in the digital space and must be prioritized to build trust, loyalty, and repeat business. By following these steps, you can create an online marketing strategy that helps you reach your target audience, achieve success with your business goals, and grow your business over time

This book further explores expanding and scaling your business, including using strategic partnerships, outsourcing, and diversifying your products or services. It also provides tips on keeping your business booming, including staying current on industry trends and continually improving customer experience.

Expanding a business requires more than just offering goods and services. You must also know and comply with local, state, and federal laws and regulations. Investing in the right people

Conclusion

and technology can help your business reach new levels of success. By satisfying customer needs, staying compliant with regulations, monitoring your online reputation, and leveraging partnerships, you can take your business to the next level.

Employing KPI tracking software has proven to be a powerful tool for businesses, offering insight into trends and patterns and unlocking creative thinking. This is essential for any business looking to optimize operations, achieve greater success, and exceed customer expectations. It can help set actionable goals, increase motivation and productivity, and provide benchmarks to maintain steady progress.

To maximize profits, businesses should focus on back-end sales and upselling strategies. This involves offering customers complementary or upgraded products just before they complete their purchase. By doing this, businesses can increase their profits significantly by capitalizing on loyal customers who already trust and value the product or service. Additionally, offering special incentives to encourage customer loyalty will build stronger relationships and create a steady stream of repeat buyers.

In conclusion, The Online Business Academy for Beginners offers valuable insights into starting and building a profitable online business. The book covers a wide range of topics, from legal requirements to marketing strategies, and provides practical advice on managing finances, expanding your business, and keeping it successful. It is a comprehensive guide that can help beginners get started and experienced entrepreneurs take their businesses to the next level.

If you've been considering starting an online business, this book is a must-read. With the knowledge and tools provided, you can launch your online business with confidence and build it into a successful venture.

Now that you have all the tools to start an online business, go and use them! If you enjoyed the book, please leave a review on Amazon, and share it with others who may find it helpful.

References

Allan J. (2023, February 15). *Top 12 Most Profitable Online Businesses: From Online Surveys To Affiliate Advertising.* Finances Online. https://financesonline.com/top-12-most-profitable-online-businesses-from-online-surveys-to-affiliate-advertising/

Allen M. (2019, November 4). *7 Steps to Starting a Small Business Online.* Entrepreneur. https://www.entrepreneur.com/starting-a-business/how-to-start-a-business-online/175242

Amir B. (2021, January 6). *6 Invaluable Tips for Satisfying Your Online Customers.* Entrepreneur. https://www.entrepreneur.com/growing-a-business/6-invaluable-tips-for-satisfying-your-online-customers/361355

Anil A. (2023, March 3). *Top 13 Most Profitable Niches That Really Make Money in 2023.* Blogger Passion. https://bloggerspassion.com/most-profitable-niches-list/

Bill P. (2023, March 3). *The Ultimate Guide to Hiring Virtual Assistants in 2023.* Prialto. https://www.prialto.com/blog/virtual-assistants

David R. (2022, June 9). *How to scale a successful eCommerce business with Lorna Jane.* Star Ship It. https://starshipit.com/blog-content/how-to-scale-a-successful-ecommerce-business-with-lorna-jane

Diana F. (2022, June 19). *Seven Tactics To Fund Your Online Business.* Due. https://due.com/blog/seven-tactics-fund-your-online-business/

Domenica M. (2022, September 6). *How to create a digital marketing strategy in 10 steps.* Vendasta. https://www.vendasta.com/blog/10-steps-digital-marketing-strategy/

Eric D. (2021, September 28). *How to Increase Product Value.* Five Echelon. https://fiveechelon.com/how-to-increase-product-value/

Jonas M. (2021, June 14). *10 Key Benefits Of SEO For Your Business.* Forbes. https://www.forbes.com/sites/forbesagencycouncil/2021/06/14/10-key-benefits-of-seo-for-your-business/?sh=3aad3dd03fd0

Kimanzi C. (2015, December 14). *5 Steps to Start an Online Business and Living a Much Better Life.* Entrepreneur. https://www.entrepreneur.com/starting-a-business/5-steps-to-start-an-online-business-and-living-a-much/253834

Kirsten A. (2021, October 11). *6 Types of eCommerce Business Models.* Elastic Path. https://www.elasticpath.com/blog/6-ecommerce-business-models-b2b-b2c

Kristen M. (2022, November 19). *The 25 Best Ways to Increase Your Online Presence (+Free Tools!)* Wordstream. https://www.wordstream.com/blog/ws/2021/05/17/increase-online-presence

Kristopher J. (2021, March 24). *The Importance Of Branding In Business.* Forbes. https://www.forbes.com/sites/forbesagencycouncil/2021/03/24/the-importance-of-branding-in-business/?sh=4eda2ad667f7

Kyle A. (2023, January 12). *4 Reasons Why Building Customer Relationships is Especially Important Now.* Octane AI. https://www.octaneai.com/blog/customer-relationships

Leonardus N. (2023, February 27). *I Bought a Domain, Now What? 7 Steps to Have a Successful Website.* Hostinger. https://www.hostinger.com/tutorials/i-bought-a-domain-name-now-what

References

Maria B. (2021, January 11). *5 Ways to Analyze and Understand Your Online Sales.* TMC Net. https://www.tmcnet.com/topics/articles/2021/01/11/447630-5-ways-analyze-understand-online-sales.htm

Mitch D. (2021, September 20). *How to Create a Unique Online Value Proposition.* Full Surge. https://www.fullsurge.com/blog/how-to-create-a-unique-online-value-proposition

Steve N. & Rosalie M. (2022, July 26). *How to Write a Business Plan, Step by Step.* Nerd Wallet. https://www.nerdwallet.com/article/small-business/business-plan

Thomas J. L. (2022, October 19). *Entrepreneurial Mindset: 20 Ways to Think like an Entrepreneur.* Oberlo. https://ng.oberlo.com/blog/entrepreneurial-mindse t

Zac J. (2023, February 21). *How Much Does It Cost to Start an Online Business?* Business. https://www.business.com/articles/costs-of-starting-online-business/

Zaryn D. (2014, March 21). *How the Internet Has Changed Everyday Life.* BBVA Open Mind. https://www.bbvaopenmind.com/en/articles/internet-changed-everyday-life/amp/

Made in the USA
Las Vegas, NV
14 September 2023